Until I Smile at You

**How one girl's heartbreak electrified
Frank Sinatra's fame!**

Ruth Lowe
Painting by Charles Pachter

Until I Smile at You:

How one girl's heartbreak electrified Frank Sinatra's fame!

by
Peter Jennings

with contributions by
Tom Sandler

Castle Carrington Publishing
Victoria, BC
Canada

2020

Until I Smile at You
How one girl's heartbreak electrified
Frank Sinatra's fame!

Copyright © Peter Jennings and Tom Sandler, 2020

First published in paperback in 2020
Cover Design: Peter Jennings
Photographs and illustrations: © Tom Sandler unless otherwise noted

ISBN: 978-1-990096-03-7 (paperback)
ISBN: 978-1-990096-04-4 (Kindle-book)
ISBN: 978-1-990096-05-1 (Smashwords e-book)

Published in Canada by
Castle Carrington Publishing
www.castlecarringtonpublishing.ca
Victoria BC
Canada

Visit the authors at:
www.peterjennings.me
www://tomsandler.photoshelter.com/gallery-list
More about this book at: www.untilismileatyou.com

EARLY REVIEWS

As usual, you've taken us on a compelling journey and I truly enjoyed my time reading this. Written history rarely takes us to the spark of artistic invention… Thankfully, one such journey to the source of artistic genius is at hand. What's new in Peter Jennings' book "Until I Smile at You" are the people he's found to take us to the heart of such genius—the Sinatras, (Nancy and Frank Jr.), Ruth's sister and son, Dorsey and scores of other witnesses to the story. It's as if Jennings has convened a dinner party in Ruth's honour and everybody shows up to offer a take on a landmark Great American Songbook tune. I mean, even Tim Rice, Bernie Taupin, David Clayton-Thomas, and Chuck Granata attend to ensure that Ruth's song, Frank's rendition, and their genius are given their due. While it's art born in tragedy, it's also a story that delivers triumph.

Ted Barris
noted author of 21 books

It was wonderful to pursue Ruth Lowe's life through your book and realize what a talented lady she was. Hats off to you for bringing her story to life and giving her the credit she deserves today. I think you have truly nailed it

SW

You are able to capture a wonderful profile of a really neat and interesting person and the way you tell the story enriches the narrative. It gave me a whole bunch of insight into the music industry of that era. It's a great story, well told. It is a captivating read.

JRM

I know you were concerned about not overdoing the *information*. Don't worry, there's not a dull phrase in this book. It's riveting. Having the experts talk about Ruth's music really puts it in perspective.

CT

It's a well-written and thoroughly researched account of her life.

Douglas Richmond, Editor
House of Anansi Press

Very well written. I'm sure it will appeal to music lovers of all ages. A great tribute to Ruth Lowe. Tom's tribute to his Mom brought tears... "don't want Mom's story forgotten." You caused me to laugh out loud in parts and tear up in others. You've written from your heart and your love of music. Wonderfully written. Thanks for sharing.

JB

It is so Canadian that someone as advanced, influential, and gifted as Ruth flies under our radar. If she had been a hockey player performing at this level, she would be a national hero. If this tome doesn't raise her visibility nothing will. It is a captivating read.

RM

And this from musician/writer Jack Hutton (who played piano when Tom Sandler sang "I'll Never Smile Again" to a standing ovation crowd):

Hi Tommy:
I am so #$%^ proud of what you are doing to promote your mother's memory and the song that Tommy Dorsey recorded with a skinny Italian-American kid whose last name ended with a vowel. I'm looking forward to reading all about it and helping to promote it through our media up here. Please keep me posted all the way.

JH

OTHER BOOKS BY PETER JENNINGS

Shark Assault: An Amazing Story of Survival
www.sharkassault.com

Being Happy Matters
www.beinghappymatters.life

Pushing The Boundaries: How To Get More Out of Life
www.pushingtheboundaries.life

Behind The Seams
www.marilynbrooks.com

For Want Of 40 Pounds
www.forwantof40pounds.com

DEDICATION

This book is inscribed to those people around the world who recognize the allure of a beautiful song

Beautiful music resonates. Especially when it has to do with heartache. Most people are destined to experience some anguish in their life. Unfortunately, that's just the way things are. But no matter how old you are or what generation you're from, what can help you break through is a song.

"I'll Never Smile Again" is such a song. A timeless song.

It's a song written by a sorrowful young lady from Canada that literally electrified Frank Sinatra's fame.

It's a tune that's been played millions of times.

And it's got lots more revolutions in its future.

Contents

FOREWORD

The Perfect Song

Nancy Sinatra

Figure 1: Frank and Nancy (age 3½)
Photo: Sinatra Family Archive

I'm too young to remember when Ruth Lowe wrote "I'll Never Smile Again"—I was born two months after my dad recorded it in 1940, with Tommy Dorsey and the Pied Pipers. But I do have warm memories of him performing the song and how much he adored it. It became a touchstone for me, as I've always associated it with those wonderful early years when mom and dad were first married, and he was a young crooner starting out on his magnificent journey.

We lived in Hasbrouck Heights, New Jersey then, and on weekends we'd drive up to the Dorsey farm in Bernardsville, where Tommy (my godfather) would host the entire band and their families for big, fun outings. On Sunday, everyone would gather in the ballroom to listen and watch as the band performed a live broadcast over NBC radio. No broadcast was complete without "I'll Never Smile Again," which became one of the band's signature ballads. Who could possibly resist those soft, tender vocals by Frank, Jo Stafford, and the Pipers?

There's a reason why "I'll Never Smile Again" has endured: it was a perfect song, interpreted by the perfect singer, at the perfect time. It was a meeting of honesty—the fundamental quality my dad possessed—and the heartfelt, plaintive cry of a young, grieving widow. Ruth's lyrics bespoke *vulnerability*, and as America became immersed in the war, they became deeply meaningful to millions of girls on the home front. Lyrically, "I'll Never Smile Again" stands alongside the very best of songs. It's as ingenious as what Oscar Hammerstein II crafted for "All the Things You Are," "The Song is You," and "The Folks Who Live on the Hill"—songs that *obliquely* say "I love you."

Not surprisingly, "I'll Never Smile Again" became dad's first chart hit. It helped bolster his confidence and gave his career the boost it needed. He rerecorded the song twice (in 1959, for his somber ballad album *No One Cares* and again in 1965, for *A Man and his Music*), and always spoke lovingly—*reverentially*—of its importance.

Although we never discussed it, I can't imagine that my dad wasn't impressed by Ruth Lowe's moxie. There were only a handful of women writing pop songs in the 1940s, and Frank surely admired how Ruth—a housewife from Canada—had managed to break into such a competitive, male-dominated business. My father was relentless in his support and encouragement of those in the minority—particularly if they were his friends. More than this, he was extraordinarily loyal. He admired Ruth and considered her a friend. When you think about it, she was in superb company: Ruth was the only female songwriter to custom-write songs for Frank Sinatra, standing tall alongside three titans of the craft: Sammy Cahn, Jule Styne, and Jimmy Van Heusen—his long-time "personal" writers. That alone tells us how highly dad regarded Ruth and her talent.

One of his first tasks upon leaving the Dorsey band in 1942 was to commission Ruth to write him a new theme song. Pop's work on radio was crucial to his going solo, and he recognized how essential a unique musical signature was. To open his radio programs, Frank chose a Cole Porter favorite, "Night and Day." To end each show on a sweet, wistful note, he selected "Put Your Dreams Away (for Another Day)," newly written by Ruth Lowe, Paul Mann, and Stephan Weiss. Both songs—a Porter chestnut and a custom-written contemporary song—became Sinatra standards that my dad sang on radio and television programs well into the 1980s.

"Put Your Dreams Away" has always been personal to all the Sinatras. It's not insignificant that my siblings and I chose "Put Your Dreams Away" as the closing song for Dad's funeral service in 1998: when I began my weekly radio program at Sirius-XM radio in 2007, the first thing I did was establish the song as our closing theme.

Ruth must have been extraordinarily proud of her accomplishments and gratified that Frank Sinatra helped turn her masterpieces into classics. I'm sure she'd be equally proud of the loving treatment that *her* story—which extends well beyond the songs she wrote—is finally receiving. I'm grateful for Ruth's invaluable contribution to the Sinatra legacy and for my dad's knack for *always* choosing the right tunes, "I'll Never Smile Again" and "Put Your Dreams Away" among them.

God Bless you, Ruth—and sleep warm…

Nancy Sinatra
Los Angeles, CA
September 2019

PREFACE

Behind the Words

Peter Jennings

Seems to me that I ought to start this story with a confession. And it's this: I'm a steadfast fan of the Great American Songbook. Always have been. So, you might want to take that as fair warning: there will be some bias in this book.

Now, for those of you who are pining for punk rock or revelling in the latest rap rave, I should explain: we're talking here about a group of literally thousands of tunes known as "Standards." If per chance you're new to this, you need to know that the Great American Songbook is the oeuvre of the most important popular songs from the 1910s to the 1960s that were created by George Gershwin, Cole Porter, Irving Berlin, Jerome Kern, Harold Arlen, Johnny Mercer, Richard Rodgers, and so many more. They represent the important and influential popular songs and jazz tunes from the 20th century. Most were created for Broadway shows and Hollywood films.

These are songs that have never really gone out of style. But then again, why should they? I mean, we're talking composers and lyricists who knew how to turn a tune into lilting lessons of love sung by the likes of Frank Sinatra, Bing Crosby, Ella Fitzgerald, Al Jolson, Louis Armstrong, Billie Holiday, Judy Garland, Mel Tormé, Sarah Vaughan, and so many others—the Adeles and Bruno Marses and Justin Beibers of their time. And if indeed you *are* new to this, you may be asking why you haven't heard about this genre before. Well, that's because a couple of guys set out to kill it.

First was Mitchell William "Mitch" Miller, a chap who grew up playing a pretty fair oboe and who elevated himself into being the A&R (Artist & Repertoire) man for Columbia Records. As a record producer, Miller gained a reputation for gimmickry. His relentlessly cheery arrangements and his penchant for novelty material—for example, "Come on-a My House" (Rosemary Clooney), "Mama Will Bark" (Frank Sinatra)—has drawn criticism from serious admirers of traditional pop music. In fact, music historian Will Friedwald (see page 51 for his comments on Ruth's music), a man for whom I have great respect, wrote in his book, *Jazz Singing*,[1]

> *Miller exemplified the worst in American pop. He first aroused the ire of intelligent listeners by trying to turn—and darn near succeeding in turning—great artists like Sinatra, Clooney, and Tony Bennett into hacks. Miller chose the worst songs and put together the worst backings imaginable—not with the hit-or-miss attitude that bad musicians traditionally used, but with insight, forethought, careful planning, and perverted brilliance.*

Ouch!

The second guy—the accomplice to the intended slaying of the Great American Songbook—was Robert Zimmerman. You may know him better as Bob Dylan. He set out to change the timbre of music through writing and singing folk songs that connected with a younger generation who did not link to their parents' style. Result: the Great American Songbook faded with the sunset, just like it was blowin' in the wind.

Now, before you fire off letters to my publisher, I'm not dissing Dylan. I like his stuff. But it's a matter of public record that folk songs helped kill standards. That's all I'm saying. And it's likely worth noting that when rock and roll finally arrived in the 1950s with Bill Haley and Elvis Presley, no less than famed showman

---

[1] *Jazz Singing: America's Great Voices from Bessie Smith to Bebop and Beyond*, Will Friedwald, Da Capo Press 1996, page 211.

and songwriter Billy Rose would go on record to the U.S. Congress about "corruption in the record industry."

But surprise: a renewed popular interest in the Songbook has led a growing number of rock and pop singers to take interest and issue their own interpretations. It started with Linda Rhonstat (she of the "Stone Ponies") who hired arranger extraordinaire Nelson Riddle to fashion a series of "standards" albums for her that have since been followed by Rod Stewart, Annie Lennox, K.D. Lang, George Michaels, Lady Gaga (with none other than Tony Bennett), et al. And, oh yeah, Bob Dylan himself, who's released a couple of albums of standards associated with Sinatra. What goes around...

Apparently, there's breath left in the ole Songbook yet.

OK, with that out of the way, let's move on to the book you're reading, *Until I Smile At You*. Strange name for a non-fiction work? Not so when you realize that what I began seeking with this anthology was not so much the smile, but the story behind the smile. That of the late Ruth Lowe who wrote the song that put a wiry kid named Sinatra on the map. You see, as I recently confessed to Tom Sandler, Ruth's son and a well-known photographer, I have for years hummed or whistled the tune to "I'll Never Smile Again" nonchalantly, and without realizing it, in the background as I go about my daily routine. With absolutely no warning at all, this infectious melody has become my go-to tune, the one I apparently fall back on easily and without restraint as I seek a melodic background to the daily grind.

But surely this alone fails to qualify me as Ruth Lowe's biographer. There must be a greater connection. And, indeed, there is.

I recently became aware that Mr. Sandler makes Toronto his home—that city being my former bailiwick where I lived and breathed before moving away from the Big Smoke a few years ago. With 2015 being heralded as the 100th anniversary of Sinatra's birth, I had planned a fund-raising concert to commemorate the singer out in the boonies where I live. A friend told me about Sandler, and I arranged to meet him to share my plans for this event. We hit it off easily and, to cut to the chase, I not only convinced Tommy (he was named by his mom for Tommy Dorsey, after all) to appear with me so I could interview him along with his memories and priceless heritage photos, but—wait for it—I actually convinced him to sing "the song" live before our audience. He'd never done this before, and, indeed, it took some persuasion. But Tommy came through, sat for the interview, and then stood nervously before an appreciative audience who broke into a standing ovation at his recitation's completion. It was a magic moment.

Figure 2: Tom—I'll Never Smile Again

Later that evening, as the musicians who had participated gathered at my place for drinks to celebrate our accomplishment, Tommy told me he'd been trying for years to get a book written about his mom. "You're a writer," he told me, "and you love the

Great American Songbook. And you love mom's song. Could there be anyone better to write her story?" He looked down for a moment, then eyed me straight on and said six words I'll never forget. "I don't want mom's story forgotten." As I considered this, he added: "I now know I've met the man to ensure her life will continue to shine."

The dawn came up like thunder, and I expected Tommy might ignore the revelry of the night before. But no, he was on it like a cur savouring a bone. "Peter, I've thought it out. You're the man! You're the one to write mom's story." He looked me in the eye: "Will you do it?"

It took—oh gosh, maybe two seconds—for me to reply, "Tommy, if you're keen, count me in. I'd be honoured. It's a writer's dream!"

Sandler then explained he had links to people I could meet who would fill in the blanks about Ruth Lowe's life. Folks like Ruth's kid sister, 96-year-old Muriel Cohen, whom he knew would be happy to meet with me and share her memories. And Seymour Schulich, legendary billionaire philanthropist who'd learned his trade at the feet of Tommy's father, Nat Sandler, Ruth's second husband. And with these luminaries, it was clear we were just scratching the surface.

OK, enough said. *"Until I Smile at You"* is the result of this serendipitous experience. And it's about time too, since the full story of Ruth Lowe's amazing life—and the legacy she left for the world—has never been told until now.

And there's one last thing. Having immersed myself in research about Ruth Lowe, having talked with so many people who knew and admired her, and after spending time with Tommy sharing what an amazing person his mom was, I feel cheated that I never got to meet her, to know her. How wonderful it would have been to spend time in her company, being part of that realm she occupied. But, alas, like you, I will have to satisfy myself by getting close to Ruth Lowe in the pages that follow.

Now, just before we get to our story, a note about the people I talked with in compiling this book. Chapter 8 features commentary from several well-known song writers, performers, and entertainers. I sought them out and interviewed them to gauge their impressions of Ruth Lowe's talent. Why? It still blows me away that "I'll Never Smile Again" eclipsed all other songs of the time with such power. Not that Ruth's effort is undeserving of huge commendation: it is an absolute masterpiece that endures to this day. But the famous Dorsey/Sinatra version recorded in 1940 is filled with slow-moving anguish. Chart that against the upbeat songs that competed for dominance that year and you have to wonder: how could heartbreak out-sell the verve, vigor, and gusto of virtually every other tune of the day? I figured there was only one way to solve this poser, and that was to ask people whose knowledge of music is more profound than mine. In short, their opinions solidified what is fact, just as Nancy Sinatra says in the Foreword, "It was a perfect song, interpreted by the perfect singer at the perfect time."

I'd like to publicly thank each of the participants who talked with me and shared their enthusiasm for Ruth's ability to write such a classic piece. Each of them was only too happy to go on the record and contribute to this, the only complete record of Ruth Lowe's amazing life. Your thoughts and conclusions make this story so much more thorough. (Source information is covered in the Acknowledgment section at the end of this book.)

Ok, read on. Tom Sandler and I hope you enjoy this story as much as we did composing it.

INTRODUCTION

A Song Unfinished

Tom Sandler

*"Tommy, do something normal with your
life...go into show biz!"*

Ruth Lowe Sandler

Yup, that's what my mom told me as I was searching about trying to decide what adventures life should take me on. Not "Become a doctor" or "Study law" or "How 'bout Accounting?" Nope. "Go into show biz!" Only my mom could have said such a thing. "Something normal," the world of show biz having offered her so much that it just seemed second nature to her. I am so proud of my mom, who she was and her great musical accomplishments.

In an era of female empowerment, with so many talented women reaching out to share their lives, here is the lady who led them all. Ruth Lowe: the Canadian who has been called one of the "Architects of the American Ballad." Her music has been recorded by every legend of jazz and is still being recorded today. Even more amazing, we are talking about a woman who, in the 1930s, lost everything. Everything, that is, except her courage, her talent, the love for her family, and her will to survive.

She has always been an inspiration to me with her gift of music and her vaudeville take on life. Mom touched my heart. She moved me in so many ways and filled me up with her music. She shared those gifts with me and everyone she met. She opened up and let people in, to smile, to cry, to be who they were.

"Go into show biz!" indeed. You know, mom faced dangers and heartbreaks during a time when there was nothing but... dangers and heartbreaks: the Depression years. She became the sole supporter of her family, which included my aunt and my grandmother, after her father died. Eventually, when she went on the road, she still took care of them, sending back money, clothes, whatever they needed. She was a great daughter, a loving mom, an amazing grandmother, an astonishing musician, and a loyal friend. Most of all, Mom was a true artist. She always played her piano at home: it was her best friend, the music was always there to fill her heart, making her smile as she always did for me and for everyone she met. She understood the joys and celebrations of life, while at the same time being such a generous and loving spirit who touched the hearts of people throughout the world with her songs and the incredible story behind writing "I'll Never Smile Again." I was so lucky to have a mother who was successful on so many fronts: music, family, and personal. She was a woman who was not afraid to open her heart to feel and share the love that we all need so badly. She led by her heart, knowing that everything else would follow. And wherever she went, whoever she met, they loved and respected her, being blown away by her charm and warmth.

Ruth Lowe was loved and respected by the greatest musicians in the world, whose careers were advanced greatly after they covered her music. She still is (as you'll learn in this book). The standard she composed is, as they say in music, a song that will last forever in the world as well as in people's hearts. Not many artists in history have done that.

Having lived such an amazing life, Mom passed away in 1981 after fighting cancer for 10 years. She died alone in the hospital on a cold, dark January night, her battle finally over. She was only 66, such a bright light extinguished way too early. I often think her life was like a song unfinished.

Mom, I can't find the words to say how much we love you and miss you. How much you added to the quality of our lives. How much you sacrificed for us all. You were, and will always be, my heroine. And you gave us a gift that can't be measured: your music and your love.

I hope you all enjoy this book—until I smile at "you", Ma.

PART ONE

Chapter One

What Goes Around...

"We've been working on this *Canadiana* album for a year now," says George Koller. He's mother-henning around the studio, making sure everything is just so before the main act arrives. The main act, in this case, being the immortal David Clayton-Thomas, one of the most recognizable voices in music as lead singer with Blood, Sweat & Tears and famed for his composition "Spinning Wheel", now enshrined in the Songwriter's Hall of Fame. The guy's only sold, like, 40 million records.

"We've got 13 tunes planned for the album, and they're all Canadian," Koller states proudly. "But here's the thing: everyone expects a record like this to have stuff by Lightfoot and Joni Mitchell, Sarah McLachlan, Leonard Cohen, Shirley Eikard. But how many people know that one of the biggest songs of all time was written—words and music—by a Canadian girl back in 1939?"

That girl would be Ruth Lowe. And while she was assumed by many to be American, because she was living in the U.S., having married a lad from Chicago, Ruthie hailed originally from Toronto.

"And I'll bet you didn't know this," George adds. "DCT and Ruth share some amazing similarities. Think about it. Both of them are Canadian. Both are Grammy Award winners. Both enjoyed huge musical success with tunes in the U.S. and around the world. Both moved to the U.S. Both returned home to Canada. She wrote 'I'll Never Smile Again' and he sings it on the new album." He stops, looks up and smiles at this compendium of parallels.

Meanwhile, the studio gets busy as various musicians arrive. Coffees are poured, instrument cases are opened.

And then, David Clayton-Thomas himself ambles through the studio doors.

"Waz happenin?" he calls out to no one in particular. "Gonna make some magic today?"

DCT opens a briefcase full of lyric sheets and begins setting up on the singer's podium.

"So, what was your criteria in choosing tracks for this album?" he's asked.

"Well, we looked at what we could bring to each song, you know, to give it a different sense," he explains. "'I'll Never Smile Again' was always on the list. Not just because it's such a great song, but because we wanted the album to have a historical presence, not just modern rock songs."

Indeed, DCT's background includes immersing himself in the jazz and blues scene as a younger man, attracted by superb musicians like Oscar Peterson, Moe Koffman, and Lenny Breau. He's no stranger to tunes like the one Ruth Lowe wrote.

And let the record show that David Clayton-Thomas is no shrinking violet in his enthusiasm for her song. "We're doing something rather unorthodox with this recording," he explains. "Going right back to a retro version. You know, The Willows (an all-girl singing trio) filling in for the Pied Pipers. Russ Little's doing a little Tommy Dorsey tribute on the trombone. Going to recapture that sound, that spirit of the Tommy Dorsey/Frank Sinatra style. Going to be a beautiful track. Absolutely one of the best tracks on the album, no question."

Back to Ruth. It's more than intriguing that competing songs in 1940 all hailed from Broadway and Hollywood musicals, so they were unfailingly up-beat, happy-go-lucky lilts. And then, along comes her sad lament that rockets to the top of the charts.

"What's with that?" Clayton-Thomas is asked.

"Well, you've got a great tune and wonderful lyrics," he says. "And you know what: quality always comes through. Doesn't matter whether it's happy or sad. 'I'll Never Smile Again' is well-written. It has a tune that sticks in your mind once you've heard it. I can't imagine it being a better song. Neither could Frank

Sinatra: he said it many times publicly. 'I'll Never Smile Again' was the one he loved to sing the most in concert."

George Koller is ready to try making a record. "Two minutes," he calls out. Meanwhile, DCT is contemplating Ruth Lowe's life after "I'll Never Smile Again": how she shunned the limelight and returned to Canada.

"I made a similar decision," he states. "I'd lived in New York for almost 40 years. But in 2005, I found myself the last remaining member of BS&T. Half the guys coming into the band weren't even born when we started it, and I just got fed up. We were almost like a tribute band at that point, with me as the last man standing. They were never going to make another record. Making millions on the road was their style, so who wants to go into the studio? Me!! So, I came home to Toronto."

And when you hear David Clayton-Thomas sing "I'll Never Smile Again" on *Canadiana*, you'll be glad he did.

But how is it that a guy who began life as a homeless street kid and developed into one of the most recognizable voices in music is in a studio recording a lament written nearly 80 years before?

Ah. Now in that, we have a story.

Chapter Two

The Sentimental Gentleman of Swing

To understand how an inexperienced young lady from Canada could take the world by storm by doing the impossible—writing words and music to a heart-gushing requiem that would give young Frank Sinatra's career a rocket boost into the stratosphere—well, you need to get your head around the times back then. So, let's take a little meander down memory lane.

It's the 1930s and 40s, and music rules like no time before or since. The big bands of the era are filling the ears, eyes, and minds of just about everybody who will listen, regardless of race, creed, or color. From Glenn Miller to Benny Goodman to Artie Shaw to Count Basie to Jimmie Lunceford to Duke Ellington to the aggregation led by the guy they would come to term "the General Motors of the Band Business"—Tommy Dorsey—it is a time of musical rewards all around.

This Dorsey was an interesting cat, an American original. Born in November of 1905, he'd made his entree into the music biz because his father, a coal miner, recognized mining offered a dead-end future and stated, "I'll do anything to keep my sons out of the mines." And so, the stage was set for Tom to join his older brother Jim in establishing their musical talents by playing in local concerts and parades. Jimmy would soon gravitate to reed

Figure 3: Tommy Dorsey

instruments, while Tommy came to favour brass.

So, what was the relationship like between the siblings? "Well, it was a very complicated, very Irish, kind of thing," says Peter Levinson, author of *Tommy Dorsey: Livin' in a Great Big Way*.

"Very close as brothers, and yet feuding and fighting, and when I say fighting, I mean fist fighting, often," Levinson comments. "And if anyone came to separate the two, then the two brothers would fight that person. It was their own fight. No one else was supposed to get in between them at any time. There was a great respect, a great love, but also a great jealousy." [2]

Now, Tommy Dorsey was a piece of work. Levinson tells us that he drank too much, he was a womanizer—even being suspicious of his own wife while he was cheating on her—and there were many other things not to like about the man. "But he also had tremendous charm and he could take care of people," the author says.

And with Frank Sinatra, it was a tumultuous relationship between him and Dorsey from the start. Still, the singer learned a great deal from his mentor.

Levinson:

> There's a key quote that I got from Vince Falcone, who played piano for Sinatra during the '70s and later in the '80s, and who said to me, "You know," Frank said, "The two most important people in my life have been my mother and Tommy Dorsey. [3]

It should be said that both the Dorsey boys knew their way around a bottle of hooch. But Tommy experienced an attack of appendicitis and hospitalization in June 1933. Reading the tea

---

[2] *Tommy Dorsey: Livin' in a Great Big Way*, Peter J. Levinson, copyright © 2005, reprinted with permission of Da Capo Press an imprint of Hachette Publishing Group Inc.
[3] See footnote 2 above

leaves, he vowed to stop drinking, an oath from which his older brother abstained, and the two musicians went their separate ways.

Tommy, who by now went with the nicknames Mac and TD, was a driven soul. It didn't take long for "Tommy Dorsey and his Orchestra" to make their debut in October 1935 at the French Casino in New York. Soon, he'd signed a recording contract with RCA for its Victor label.

Dorsey dreamed big and was not afraid to spend money to get to the top. He hired singer Jack Leonard and trumpet player-arranger, Axel Stordahl (who would go on to fame with Frank Sinatra as the singer's full-time arranger after he left the Dorsey band in 1943). Soon, Tommy's orchestra was selling records, making big impressions with several number one hits and being featured on radio and in personal appearances, including starring gigs on NBC's radio program *The Magic Key of RCA*. By July 1937, the Dorsey band had become the headliner on the new *Raleigh-Kool Show*, introducing Tommy as "That Sentimental Gentleman of Swing."

Fast forward to the summer of 1939: TD is firmly established. His engagement at the coveted Hotel Pennsylvania in New York has justifiably positioned him at the top of the top. But Dorsey is restless. Yes, his popularity has become significant: yet he's still always on the lookout for new and challenging directions. "Being competitive was not enough," according to Dennis M. Spragg, writing in the University of Colorado's Glenn Miller Archive. "He wanted to win. He wanted to be number one."

Tommy was smart enough to accept that great singers could make his band more appealing to the masses. And so, hearing that young Frank Sinatra had joined trumpeter Harry James and his orchestra and was beginning to show promise, he kept his eye on the ambitious kid. As James Kaplan tells us in his biography *Frank: The Voice,* "Harry James was a hot artist: a hepcat, a weed-puffing wild man. He was also a strangely self-defeating character—alcoholic, remote, and persistently broke.

That summer, he lost everything he had in a settlement over an auto accident."

James had offered Sinatra a contract of $75 a week (neglecting to reveal that there might be some weeks when he wouldn't have the dough to pay up). He also wanted his new protégée to change his brand: Sinatra was too "Eye-talian." "How 'bout Frankie Satin?" the bandleader suggested. "It'll go good with that nice smooth voice of yours."

However, Frank Sinatra stood firm, commenting years later, "Can you imagine? Is that a name or is that a name? 'Now playing in the lounge, ladies and gennulmen, the one an' only Frankie Satin.' If I'd've done that, I'd be working cruise ships today."

Kaplan:

> *The Voice—might as well start capitalizing it here—was simply working its spooky subliminal magic. Did it help that the singer was clearly in need of a good meal, that his mouth was voluptuously beautiful, that his electric-blue eyes were attractively wide with fear and excitement, that he knowingly threw a little catch, a vulnerable vocal stutter, into his voice on the slow ballads? It helped. It whipped into a frenzy the visceral excitement that his sound had started. But the sound came first. There was simply nothing like it.*[4]

TD's always sharp antennae told him that James was having a hard time making a go of it. As it happened, both his band and James' were booked into Chicago at the same time, so Tommy schemed to meet with Sinatra. His pitch was simple: $125 a week versus James' $75 stipend. For Sinatra, whose wife Nancy was pregnant with their first child, the raise would be welcome. But not

---

[4] *Frank: The Voice*, James Kaplan, Anchor Books (part of the Knopf Doubleday Publishing Group), 2001.

nearly as encouraging as riding up that elevator of renown to singing with the top band in the land. Now, *that* was something money couldn't buy.

Around the same time, Mac offered employment to a Southern California singing group known as "the Pied Pipers."

With the addition of this vocal quartet, plus Sinatra, Tommy Dorsey knew he was now poised to make history.

Chapter Three

The Art of the Record

It's the afternoon of May 23rd, 1940. Tommy Dorsey enters the RCA recording studio in Rockefeller Centre, New York City, ready to make a record of distinction. He's one tough task master. Standing five ten, ramrod-straight, impeccably dressed, he looks more like a math teacher than a popular band leader who spends most of his life on the road. And man, can he play that trombone!

"He could do something with a trombone that no one had ever done before," stated clarinettist extraordinaire Artie Shaw. "He made it into a singing instrument. Before that it was a blatting instrument."

On this fine spring day, Dorsey has chosen to do battle with a certain song by using a stripped-down unit from his big band. He calls them "The Sentimentalists," so named from the leader's theme song "I'm Getting Sentimental Over You" by Ned Washington and George Basman, and a descendent of Dorsey's "Clambake Seven," a band within a band that he'd formed to play small group jazz instrumentals with novelty vocals.

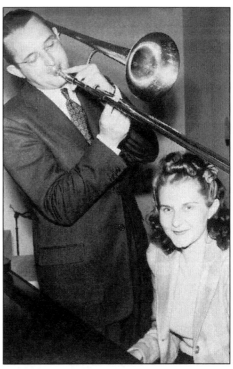

The Sentimentalists are joined by the Pied Pipers singing quartet.

Dorsey had actually tried to record this number—"I'll Never Smile Again"—a month

Figure 4: Tommy Dorsey and Ruth

earlier. It was at the end of a session with just a few minutes left on the clock, but they didn't enjoy much success and abandoned the effort. This time, it'll be different: TD's going to let his sax player, Fred Stulce, do the arrangement, keeping it simple, classy. They're going to slow it down. Way down.

And he's decided to put the spotlight on his new boy singer.

For his part, the skinny, big-eared Italian-American kid with the hot, seductive voice that trembles, is not looking to record just any song. After all, 25-year-old Frank Sinatra's been in the recording studio before, working with the Harry James orchestra. No, this time—now that he's elevated himself to singing with the biggest band in the land—he's seeking to boot Bing Crosby off his pedestal, where "The Groaner" sits at the top of croonerville. And, while neither singer may know it, Bing's days in the #1 slot are numbered.

"Frank really loved music, and I think he loved singing," Jo Stafford, a member of the Pied Pipers, stated. "But Crosby, it was more like he did it for a living. He liked music well enough. But he was a much colder person than Frank. Frank was a warm Italian boy. Crosby was not a warm Irishman." In fact, Der Bingle had told lyricist Johnny Burke never to use the phrase "I love you" in any of his songs: he was smart enough to know he just couldn't carry off that kind of emotion. He was also wise with the competition that was brewing: "Frank Sinatra is the kind of singer who comes along once in a lifetime," he stated. "But why did it have to be *my* lifetime!?"

Sinatra explains, "Everybody was trying to copy the Crosby style—the casual kind of raspy sound in the throat. Bing was on top, and a bunch of us were trying to break in. It occurred to me that maybe the world didn't need another Crosby. I decided to experiment a little and come up with something different."

That something different is about to break out with Ruth Lowe's amazing ballad that she's managed to get into Dorsey's hands months earlier.

In the studio, TD calls for attention. He scans his ensemble carefully from behind those little round glasses that frame the master's cold eyes. He nods to Fred Stulce. And they begin making music.

Dorsey and Sinatra nail "I'll Never Smile Again" in short order on this May recording date. The song moves at a dreamy-slow tempo, starting simply with Joe Bushkin's solitary celesta rendering an introductory arpeggio. That celesta sound—eerie and ethereal, as the hammers strike the steel plates—helps make the record pensive. Then, the five-part harmony of the Pied Pipers and Sinatra join the party with a soft, vamping guitar supporting them. They sing the first stanza and a half...

> *I'll never smile again,*
> *Until I smile at you.*
> *I'll never laugh again...*[5]

But then Sinatra takes over, alone...

> *What good would it do?*

His voice quavers in that way that will come to drive the bobby-soxers wild.

Sinatra sings with such passion, such precision, exhibiting the sorrow of the song, living it, yet never over the top.

The tune is achingly slow. As columnist Mark Steyn records:

> *Not just slower than the typical big-band swingers and the fixed-tempo ballads... no, this is slower than anything else around back then. And yet it works: its eeriness is heartbreaking. Instead of the usual AABA pattern—main theme, repeat, middle section, back to main*

---

[5] I'll Never Smile Again, Words and Music by Ruth Lowe, Copyright © 1939 UNIVERSAL MUSIC CORP., Copyright Renewed, All Rights Reserved, Used by Permission, Reprinted by Permission of Hal Leonard LLC.

theme—it's ABAC. But it's so beautifully written and lushly confident you don't even notice the structure.

"He had an incomparable ear that was there right from the beginning," says James Kaplan, not only author of *Frank: The Voice* but also the follow up volume *Sinatra: The Chairman.*[6] "Sinatra was a perfectionist in the recording studio. He loved getting it right."

And get it right he did. Dorsey himself—normally taciturn and tight lipped—smiles, knowing that his sense of what makes a hit is operating in full gear. He's pleased that the attempt to record the tune from a month before has now been vanquished.

The song is sent out to the judgement of the general public as Victor 78rpm record #26628A. Hearts begin to flutter across the land and around the world.

And, before long, The Billboard responds by sending "I'll Never Smile Again" into orbit as the first ever #1 post on their chart. Four years earlier, the magazine (known simply as Billboard now) had published its first music hit parade tabulating the popularity of songs of the day, becoming America's defining measure of commercial success in the music business. By 1940, it is the "Official National Music Chart" and from this stance, The Billboard launches a song—and a career—into the stratosphere with that #1 listing.

The Dorsey/Sinatra version of "I'll Never Smile Again" stays at the head of the pack for an amazing 12 weeks, remaining forever as Tommy Dorsey's biggest hit and being selected in 1958 as one of the best pop songs of all time.

And for his contribution to that very first Number One record, the magnanimous Dorsey gives his boy singer a bonus: $25.

---

[6] Sinatra: The Chairman, James Kaplan Anchor Books (part of the Knopf Doubleday Publishing Group), 2015.

Figure 5: American Society of Composers Authors and Publishers certificate

Mark Steyn: [7]

> *The song is a breakthrough for him, and you can't put a price on that. Not long after, the Dorsey band is given a cameo in a movie called Las Vegas Nights, and Sinatra gets to sing Ruth Lowe's song again, this time on the big screen where, it should be noted, during the day they record the song, Bing Crosby happens to swing by the studio. "This Sinatra," he says to the bandleader, "Tommy, I think you've got something there.*

---

[7] *A Song for the Season*, Mark Steyn, Stockade Books, 2008, see also https://www.steynonline.com/10508/ill-never-smile-again#:~:text=Not%20long%20after%2C%20the%20band%20were%20given%20a,recorded%20it%2C%20Bing%20Crosby%20swung%20by%20the%20studio.. .

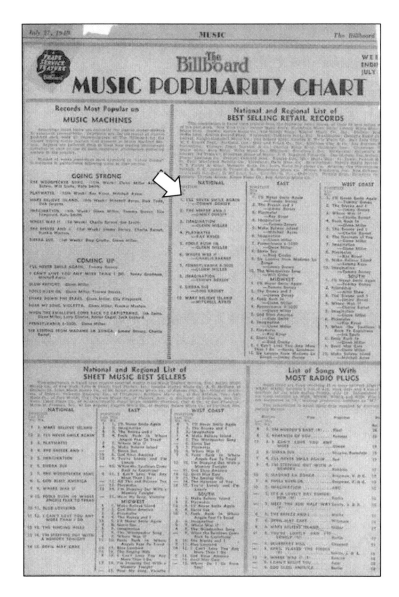

Figure 6: Number 1 on The Billboard Musical Popularity Chart

Crosby isn't the only one to take notice. Before long, every major band in the land, and most of the great singers around the world, are doing their own covers of Sinatra's song, ultimately totalling more than 150 versions.

"Dorsey was a smart cookie," explains James Kaplan. "He was the best, the most professional band leader around. He knew what was going to fly; he knew a hit when he heard one. He would not pick a song to record unless he knew it would be a hit. TD had a great ear. So, 'I'll Never Smile Again' was destined for greatness once he got his hands on it."

Frank Sinatra himself remembers hearing the melody for the first time:

> We were rehearsing on a Saturday afternoon, up at the roof of the Astor Hotel, and Tommy asked Joe Bushkin to play the song. Just the piano. I noticed that everybody suddenly was very quiet, the whole orchestra sat quietly when he played it. There was a feeling of a kind of eeriness that took place, as though we all knew that this would be a big, big hit, and that it was a lovely song.[8]

Years later, having achieved great stardom, Sinatra would continue to express his admiration for the song:

> With a tune like 'I'll Never Smile Again' and a great Tommy Dorsey arrangement, why, a mynah bird could have had a hit![9]

But then, there's this: why would such a sad elegy, as nice as the recording is, beat out competitive songs? We're talking unfailingly upbeat, happy-go-lucky pieces for the big bands of the era, designed to keep feet on the dance floor. From jazzy swingers like "In The Mood" and "Frenesi," to light-hearted lilts, such as "Pennsylvania 6-5000" and "The Woodpecker Song," to

---

[8] See footnote 6 above.
[9] See footnote 6 above.

the breezy sing-alongs "Blueberry Hill" and "You Are My Sunshine," to tony tunes like "Imagination," "All The Things You Are," and Hoagy Carmichael's immortal "Stardust," 1940 sought to distance worries of encroaching war by offering up relaxed, jaunty melodies to while away the day.

In the midst of this bright and buoyant revelry, there comes a mournful anthem that is so downcast, so built on the bonfire of anguish, a song that bespeaks such a bleak broken heart that it outclasses each and every record on the charts!

Well, stay tuned: we'll re-visit this conundrum in Chapter 8 when some very well-known musicians offer thoughts on just how and why "I'll Never Smile Again" could become such a monster, indelible hit that still resonates today.

Chapter Four

Tracing the Past

So, where did this heartbreaker come from? To answer that, we need to go back to the year Ruth Lowe's sunny personality greeted the world for the first time.

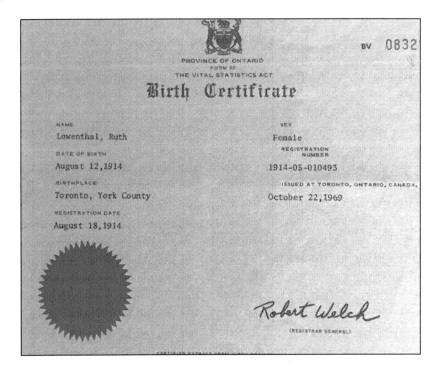

Figure 7: Ruth's birth certificate

She was born in 1914, 16 months ahead of Frank Sinatra. While no one could have predicted it, their lives would defy the odds and collide 25 years later in indelible fashion, dramatically altering each of their existences forever.

Ruth's birthplace, Toronto, is the capital of the province of Ontario and the largest city in Canada. Today, it forms part of the Greater Toronto Area with a population of six million people. "T.O." is a centre of business, finance, arts, and culture, and is recognized as one of the most multicultural and cosmopolitan cities in the world. Originally called York and established in 1793, it was incorporated as Toronto in 1834. Following the Second World War, refugees from war-torn Europe and Asian jobseekers arrived there, as well as construction labourers, particularly from Italy and Portugal, setting a standard where immigration from all parts of the world would see Toronto's population grow.

Today, we're talking about a prominent centre for music, theatre, motion picture and television production, and home to Canada's major national broadcast networks and media outlets. The city's varied cultural institutions include numerous museums and galleries, festivals and public events, entertainment districts, national historic sites, and sports activities, attracting over 25 million tourists each year. It boasts the tallest free-standing structure in the western hemisphere, the CN Tower, and is home to the Toronto Stock Exchange, the headquarters of Canada's five largest banks, and mission control for many large Canadian and multinational corporations.

But, on August 12th, 1914, Toronto was a simpler place. Baby Ruth is born there to Pearl and Samuel Lowenthal. And, as is often the custom of the time, the patriarchal name is shortened to better "anglicize" it, Lowenthal thus becoming Lowe.

As Ruth grew up, it became pretty clear that no matter where you hung your hat in the 1930s, life was never going to be easy. The Great Depression had torn the stuffing out of so many former realities and people wondered if their existences would ever be joyful again. Sumptuous meals, lavish entertainment, Charleston jubas, bathtub gin, and gay repartee had been replaced by the doggerel of smashed dreams, bitter confusion, and utter dejection.

For the Lowe family in Toronto, these times were not new, however. The four human beings didn't need a worldwide financial challenge to set them straight. They lived it, 24/7. You see, Samuel Lowe was a struggling grocer who never seemed to find real success.

"He was a gregarious, heavyset charmer," recalls Muriel Cohen, Sam's daughter, Ruth Lowe's younger sister. "He'd been born in New York City and was longer on the entrepreneurial spirit than actual business smarts. He and my mother, Pearl, seemed to always struggle to keep ends together."

Sam's life had never been serene. As a boy, he faced the fact that his family couldn't afford to raise him, so he was placed in an orphanage. His youth was spent in turmoil: he never overcame the shortfall that these early days and lack of education presented.

"Despite the nasty upbringing, he turned out to be quite a charming man," Muriel recalls about her father. "He could sing and dance and loved to entertain. Ruthie caught that bug from him, though not me. To my mother, however, he seems only to have brought a great deal of stress and heartache. He was never able to earn enough money to support his family."

Ever the speculator with an eye to making his fortune, one day, Sam announced that the four of them—Ruth, Muriel (better known as Mickey), Pearl, and him—were moving to Los Angeles. "Los Angeles!" Mickey exclaims. "We were just kids, Ruth and me. Moving away from home was a misadventure at best!"

But the family relocated from Toronto to the LA suburb of Glendale. "It was such a shock leaving our home in Canada," Mickey recalls. "Still, Glendale turned out to be a lovely place to grow up. We settled on a street featuring palm trees lined up like sentinels. It seemed there was music everywhere in town, and, on Sundays, we'd venture over to a park to hear outdoor concerts."

The Lowes lived in a small bungalow amid the lavish Californian foliage. Quite a change from Toronto's climate. But even with Glendale's booming success and the southern sun shining bright, Sam still struggled. He tried his hand at running a meat shop but failed to make enough dough to put food on the table.

"I remember I was about ten when my mom told me she and I were heading back to Toronto for a wedding," Mickey says. "I wondered even then if we'd ever come back."

Her premonition was right. While in Toronto, Pearl received a call from Sam saying he'd packed in the business and was returning east with Ruth. He sold their house in Glendale, complete with furniture, shipped the piano home, and drove back to Canada.

"It must have been quite a shock to my mother," Mickey recalls, "but, for me and Ruth, it was just another of life's passages. I guess we were used to the pandemonium by then."

Back in Toronto, Sam's persistent business exploits continued to fail. It finally wore him down. He threw in the towel.

Soon after, he died virtually penniless.

"I was only 13 when he passed away," says Mickey. "It's funny: the exact circumstances of his death were never clear. Seems on the day he died, no one knew where he was. They searched and searched. I can recall it was terrible."

Rumors of suicide would dog the family for years, Ruth, herself, never being prepared to accept that her loving father would have left her in that way.

"He would never have killed himself. He would never have left me like that," she would tell her daughter-in-law many years later.

But the reality was, Sam Lowe had been found in his car with the motor running and the garage door firmly shut.

"We'd never had a lot of money," Mickey says wistfully, "but now, with dad gone, there wasn't even the hope of cash coming in to support us."

Pearl was left to raise Ruth and Muriel on her own. If such a fate was demanding at the best of times, the Depression was the worst of times. Mind you, she had the benefit of being near her mother and sisters for support. But truth be told, there were days when Pearl wasn't convinced she'd be able to keep a roof over their heads.

Figure 8: The Lowe Family

The poor woman struggled, working as a seamstress at Tip Top Tailors. But she couldn't take the stress, not being fast enough at sewing. She had to quit. The three females were forced to move around, renting rooms in other people's houses.

"These places were so hot in the summertime," Mickey remembers. "Air conditioning wasn't yet a common reality. So, on some nights when it got really steamy, we'd just haul out and sleep on the back porch to get some cool night air."

Figure 9: Mickey, Pearl, Ruth

But, in such a sad and uncomfortable situation, at least Sam Lowe's innate musical talent had been passed along to his oldest daughter.

And it would soon pay off beyond her wildest dreams.

Meanwhile, Frank Sinatra's genesis in Hoboken, New Jersey, coming a mere year and a bit after Ruth's, almost didn't happen. He nearly perished at childbirth, surviving the ordeal being considered a miracle in itself.

December 12, 1915 sees the emergence of a baby boy weighing in at 13.5 pounds. The doctor struggles to remove such a large infant from its 19-year-old mother. He uses forceps to make it easier, thereby ripping the baby's cheek, neck, and ear, in the process puncturing the eardrum and causing severe scarring to his left cheek, neck, and ear that ran from the corner of his mouth to his jawline.

Panic sets in. The child's not breathing. The mother is in poor condition. Assuming the baby won't survive, the doc focuses on mom. But amidst the cacophony of yelling in Italian in the Monroe Street flat, Rosa, the child's grandmother, grabs the baby and holds it under the cold water tap until he suddenly starts wailing out his first song of anguish. This is how Frank Sinatra endured childbirth, entering the land of the living, to the point where he would comment later, "They weren't thinking about me, they were just thinking about my mother. They just kind of ripped me out and tossed me aside." It was a seminal moment that would affect his somewhat distant personality forever.

For its part, Frank Sinatra's birthplace is very different from Ruth Lowe's. Hoboken is a city on the Hudson River with a population of about 50,000 souls today. It's part of the New York metropolitan area and the site of Hoboken Terminal, a major transportation hub for the tri-state region.

First settled in the 17th century, and apart from its celebrity as Sinatra's birthplace, the city boasts renown as the location of the first ever recorded game of baseball, occurring in 1846 between the Knickerbocker Club and the New York Nine, at Elysian Fields. Not only that, but the first centrally air-conditioned public space in the United States was demonstrated at Hoboken Terminal. Today, the metropolis is home to the Stevens Institute of Technology (one of the oldest technological universities in the U.S.) and has the highest public transportation use of any city in the United States, with 56% of working residents using public transportation for commuting purposes each day. Hoboken, New Jersey, has also been home to several filming locations (including a wedding scene from Jennifer Aniston's film "Picture Perfect" and Elia Kazan's 1954 classic "On the Waterfront").

While Hoboken, today, is recognized for upscale shops and condominiums, it was not always thus. By the 1960s, the city had begun to deteriorate, sinking from its earlier incarnation as a lively port town into a rundown state of affairs. Turn-of-the century housing appeared shabby. Real-estate values declined. With shipbuilding cheaper overseas, industry started to fade, and single-story plants surrounded by parking lots made manufacturing and distribution more economical than old brick buildings on congested urban streets. Hobokenites began heading to the suburbs. The city was clearly in decline.

But, by the late 1970s and early 1980s, Hoboken witnessed a speculation spree, fuelled by transplanted New Yorkers and others who bought many turn-of-the-20th-century brownstones in neighborhoods that the still solid middle- and working-class population had kept intact, as well as by local and out-of-town real-estate investors who bought up 19th century apartment houses, often considered to be tenements. Hoboken began attracting artists, musicians, and upwardly mobile commuters who valued the aesthetics of residential, civic, and commercial architecture, its sense of community, and relatively cheaper rents (compared to Lower Manhattan). The Hoboken Parks Initiative municipal plan was established to create more public open spaces. The Hudson Shakespeare Company was formed and began performing "Shakespeare Mondays" at Frank Sinatra Park. Empty lots were built on. Tenements became fancy condominiums.

Overnight, it seemed, Hoboken had become a "hip" place to live. Once a blue-collar town, characterized by live poultry shops and drab taverns, the city had transformed itself into a small metropolis filled with gourmet shops and luxury dwellings. By 2016, Hoboken was ranked as the 2nd best city in New Jersey for entrepreneurs.

So, there we have it: the daughter of a poor Jewish butcher in Toronto and the son of poor Italian immigrants in Hoboken, separated by just 16 months and a mere 340 miles as the crow flies.

The similarities and differences between the two are intriguing.

Consider that Saverio Antonino Martino Sinatra, Frank's father, is almost illiterate and bounces from job to job as a fireman, boxer, and bartender. Meanwhile, Ruth's dad, Sam Lowe, tries his hand at several businesses but never quite connects with success.

The mothers are vastly dissimilar. Ruth and her sister Muriel had always regarded their mom, Pearl, as "worn down by life"; quiet, unassuming, putting up with whatever was sent her way. Yet, you would never describe Natalina Maria Vitoria Garaventa that way: "Dolly" Sinatra is a pistol: loud, foul-mouthed, smart, and very ambitious.

Figure 10: Ruth, Pearl, Mickey

Ruthie herself is innocent, trying desperately to put money on the family table by holding down a series of jobs.

But Frankie: he's a scoundrel, being arrested in his twenties and charged with carrying on with a married woman. The young man is self-absorbed, with an air of entitlement, interested only in himself and his desire to sing.

Ruth is Jewish, but not overly.

Frank's Catholic, but not overly.

Both get married in unions that don't end well: Ruth's terminating with her husband Harold's untimely death. Frank's concluding when he and Nancy divorce.

Ruth dies at 66 on January 4, 1981.

Frank defies the odds and makes it to 82, expiring on May 14, 1998. His pal Kirk Douglas offers, "Boy, heaven will never be the same!"

And consider this: even in death, the amazing unification of life forces that has existed so long between Ruth Lowe and Frank Sinatra takes a final karmic turn.

The last tune played at Ruth's funeral? "Put Your Dreams Away", the very song she had wrestled with, creating the immortal ditty overnight for her friend Frankie's radio show.

And the last tune played at Sinatra's funeral? "Put Your Dreams Away".

There you have it. If you believe there are forces out there just causing things to be, then this is your chance to celebrate.

"I chose that song specifically for the conclusion of Mom's funeral," says Tom Sandler. "It just seemed so right, so fitting, so, so perfect."

And as for the Sinatra memorial, Charles Pignone, senior vice-president of Frank Sinatra Enterprises, recalls,

> *Everybody was just sitting there and then this voice comes up. You heard the strains of the arrangement, and you'd look around and see*

Nancy Reagan, Bob Dylan, Bruce Springsteen. It was a who's who of Hollywood and New York. There was an audible gasp and then there wasn't a dry eye in the house.[10]

A surreal moment in time: the amazing merger of lives and talent had finally expired, in a way so fitting, so unforgettable.

---

[10] Charles Pignone, *The Sinatra Treasures: Intimate Photos, Mementos, and Music from the Sinatra Family Collection*, Bulfinch Books, 2004.

Chapter Five

Getting By

"She'd never taken many lessons, but Ruthie was such a talented pianist," Mickey remembers. "By the time I was a teenager, she'd dropped out of school to perform on stage and play songs in music shops. This brought some income into our nearly starving household, which really made a difference."

About those music shops...

"My family were pioneer piano makers," says Charles Heintzman, offspring of what became a celebrated Canadian piano manufacturing business whose instruments retain a reputation to this day for quality workmanship and fineness of tone. Founded by Theodor August Heintzman, a skilled piano craftsman trained in Germany, who emigrated to North America in the mid-19th century, the firm was incorporated in Toronto. The story that Heintzman worked in the same New York piano factory as Henry E. Steinway, who went on to found Steinway & Sons, is unconfirmed, but it's typical of comparisons that were often made between the instruments that the two firms produced.

"In no time, Theodor Heintzman was turning out more than 60 pianos a year," says Charles about his great grandfather. "Business boomed and that number rose to become nearly 2,000 pianos a year! So, the family opened what was a pretty nice showroom on Yonge Street in downtown Toronto."

One of the tricks of the trade in selling pianos was to hire attractive pianists who could play popular songs of the times. If you were looking to purchase an instrument, you might venture into a store and ask to hear how the piano you were considering might sound playing your chosen tune. Into such an environment young Ruth Lowe stumbled one day.

"I'm not sure if Ruth actually worked for us," says Charles. "But if it wasn't Heintzmans, it would have been a similar shop. We were all in the business of selling instruments and you did that through demonstration. We also sold sheet music, but customers wanted to hear what they were buying first. You had to demonstrate. It was that simple."

And indeed, it *was* that simple for Ruthie Lowe. Take a nice gal who's easy on the eyes, see that she can pick up a tune in no time, put her amidst glistening pianos, and Bob's your uncle!

Mind you, Ruth was just a teenager when she first went to work at the "Song Shop" where she played tunes for people who were buying sheet music.

"I think it was...darn, I can't remember when...doesn't matter really," says Mickey, searching back seventy-plus years in her memory banks. She's about to reveal the prophecy of a teacup reader.

"I really don't know why Ruthie and I went there, but anyway, this person stares at the tea leaves, looks at Ruth and says, 'One day, you will write a song that will be popular all over the world. It will be a million-dollar song. And, as a result, you'll be rich and famous.' Seriously, that's exactly what the reader said! And a year later, Ruthie lost Harold and wrote 'I'll Never Smile Again.' And you know what happened from there, don't you!"

Mickey is explaining this at 95 years of age. Frankly, she's a little embarrassed to be telling

Figure 11: Ruth at the piano

the story to her visitors, somewhat concerned they'll think she's a nut case, talking about tea leaves and all. She's prefaced the recollection about her sister by saying, "I'm not sure if I want to tell you this or not." The visitors agree that when you get to be in your 90s, there ought to be a moratorium on embarrassment. So, she has out with it, the tea reader's prediction.

Mickey shares this somewhat amazing recollection in her suite at Baycrest in Toronto on a lovely fall afternoon. Founded in 1918 as a Jewish Home for Aged, the facility has grown to include Baycrest Health Sciences, a global leader in geriatric residential living, healthcare, research, innovation, and education, with a special focus on brain health and aging. It's recognized as one of the world's top research institutes in cognitive neuroscience.

"What I like about Baycrest," Mickey says, "is that we embrace the long-standing tradition of all great Jewish healthcare institutions: improve the well-being of people in their local communities and around the globe."

Having announced this, she returns to the forecast of the tea leaves. Mickey catches the dis-believing glance of one of her visitors. "See, I told you! You think it's crazy, don't you!"

Silence hangs in the room like an uninvited visitor, broken only by Mickey adding, "Ruth laughed it off too," she states emphatically. "She thought, just as you obviously do, that it was some kind of ridiculous fantasy." Mickey pauses for effect. "But then, it all happened, didn't it? Coincidence?"

Her memory is as sharp as the proverbial tack. When asked about the early years that she and her big sister Ruth experienced—Ruth being 6 years older than Mickey—she recounts details as though it was yesterday.

"My father was a guy with a million ideas," Mickey says. "And you know, he was one of the few men who could play poker with the ladies, although that may be because he wasn't much of a card player. He was musical and comical and, for me anyway, a pleasure to be around. But not for my mother. For her, he brought stress and heartache."

"Your mother, what was she like?" Mickey is asked.

"Very quiet woman," she says quickly. "She was born in Manchester, England. One of seven children. She was but a girl when her parents decided to move the whole brood across the ocean to Canada. Now, how two immigrants originally from Russia and Poland managed with so many mouths to feed in such lean times I'll never know. Particularly with my grandfather, spending his days at a synagogue, studying, while my grandmother—Yetta—supported the family running a store selling sandwiches and other goods.

"I guess that's where my mother got her strength from because she had to keep our little family going: that was not my father's strong point. But I remember we always had a piano in the house, that's for sure. We may not have had other things, but we always had that piano. We could be poor as church mice, but there'd be the piano. And Ruthie took a few lessons up front, classical training for a very short while. Me too. But she was a natural talent. Me? Not so much. Ruth was never taught jazz: that was totally of her own invention."

"She actually studied with a Professor Zimmerman in Los Angeles when they lived there," says Penelope Peters, Professor of Music Theory, Oberlin Conservatory. "And he said Ruth could become a great concert pianist if she would continue working very hard. She'd have to have been an incredible sight-reader. To be a good sight-reader, you generally have an incredible ear."

Apparently, Ruth was not particularly good at sticking to the sheet music. She always wanted to make up her own stuff.

"I'd always heard that she was self-taught," said the late band conductor, composer, and music arranger Howard Cable. "But she certainly was an exceptional pianist."

And it was pretty apparent that the talented young lady would have to devote her talents and creative energies to putting food on the family table.

"Ruth went to work at one of those places where they sold sheet music," Mickey explains. "It was in 'The Arcade', the so-called Tin Pan Alley of Toronto. That was her livelihood. And it was the source of money for our family. I'm not even sure if she finished high school because of that. Not that this hurt her: she was smart as a whip."

For Pearl, facing life as a despondent, single, down-on-your-luck mother with two daughters, it was definitely Ruth to the rescue. Using her musical talent, Ruthie would also perform after-hours gigs with her friend, Sair Lee, seeking to bring in extra cash to feed her mom, her sister, and herself. She and Sair would do a two-piano-team act in various nightclubs. Here's the way The Billboard magazine saw them:

Figure 12: Ruth and Sair

Not very often is there anything distinctive about a double singing and piano playing combo, but in the case of Ruth Lowe and Sair Lee an exception must be made. Inasmuch as the gals not only dispense ivory tickling par excellence but give out with breezy chatter and songs that warm the insides. Their present program, which augurs fine entertainment as well as a remarkable degree of versatility by its participants, is their best recommendation. [11]

"Sair was the closest friend my sister ever had," says Mickey. "She was pretty and outgoing."

But Ruth didn't stop there. She'd work with singer George Taggart on radio station CKNC. She was staff pianist with CKLC. She sang with The Shadows, a female vocal trio. She performed with Red Hickey's dance band. Using her musical strengths to sustain her family.

And while Lady Luck may have been AWOL for Pearl Lowe, the muse was about to shine her light on Ruth.

The glimmer of hope would come about in the form of famed bandleader Ina Ray Hutton.

---

[11] *The Billboard*, September 5, 1942: 7, see https://worldradiohistory.com/hd2/IDX-Business/Music/Billboard-IDX/IDX/1942/Billboard-1942-09-05-OCR-Page-0007.pdf#search=%22ruth%20lowe%20sair%20lee%22.

Chapter Six

A Song Is Born

Born Odessa Cowan, a striking blonde hailing from Chicago, Ina Ray Hutton had been forced onto the stage as a singer and dancer before turning the tender age of eight. In this, she merely followed the family tradition, her mother, Marvel Ray, being a local pianist and entertainer. It's disputed whether or not Odessa had African American heritage, since certain census data listed her as "mulatto" and "Negro." Either way, she was described as having apple-pie looks and a jaw-dropping figure.

Like Ruth, Odessa was a bright learner. At 13, she skipped the 8th grade and went straight to high school. By the time she'd reached 18, she'd re-christened herself and was a seasoned performer. Six marriages would engulf her life over the next 45 years, but her principal claim to fame was as the spirited leader of a popular touring orchestra called "The Melodears." Jazz impresario Irving Mills put together this all-female band and in making her the leader, changed her name to Hutton (taking advantage of the notorious reputation of the Woolworth heiress Barbara Hutton) and christening his lively new discovery "The Blond Bombshell of Rhythm." She couldn't play an instrument and she didn't really conduct but, poured into a figure-hugging silver lamé gown, she wiggled around in front of the players in a vaguely rhythmic fashion. It pleased the crowds. And the band behind her was pretty good.

"I'm selling this show as a music program," she'd say with a wink, "but if curves attract an audience, so much the better."

To that end, Downbeat magazine reported that Ina Ray's stage wardrobe included 400 gowns.

That may be so, but if you're of a certain age, you'll be impressed—and surprised—that the lady's reputation had legs beyond her garments. The plot of Oscar winner Billy Wilder's 1959 film *Some Like It Hot* is based on Ina Ray's band, the movie featuring actors Jack Lemmon and Tony Curtis playing musicians escaping from witnessing a gangland murder by disguising themselves as female band players in an all-girl band. That's right: an all-girl band! The fact that Marilyn Monroe, playing Sugar, is one of their cohorts only serves to create a lively denouement to the storyline.

Figure 13: Ina Ray Hutton (with Ruth at the piano)

"I think it was 1935 when Ina Ray and Ruth came together," Mickey Cohen explains. "The Melodears were coming to Toronto for an appearance, but Ina Ray's piano player got ill. So, the band leader called ahead and told an agent she'd need to see what attractive, blonde pianists Toronto had to offer, her thinking being that she'd hire someone to fill in for the Toronto gig. Oh, and this person had to be able to arrange music as well. Of course, Ruthie had no experience doing that, but I guess she was able to fake it."

Once Ruth Lowe got word about Ina Ray Hutton's dilemma, she hied her way down to audition for the famed leader. That very day she got the job.

"I remember Ruth coming home and telling me and our mother that she'd been picked," Mickey says. "She was thrilled. And then, a few days later, she joined the band full time. And off she went."

Now, playing a gig was one thing, but heading out for an extended period on the road was quite another. Fortunately, Ruth had struck up a relationship with the Keyfetz sisters, Sylvia and Teresa, two lovely young women in Toronto who were beginning to make their mark as Canada started its ascent in the pre-WWII years. The city was fast becoming a going concern with a new downtown growing to the west of Yonge and King Streets, the administrative council had relocated to a new City Hall, the railways dominated most of the lands south of downtown, and two men at the University of Toronto had shared the Nobel Prize in Medicine for their discovery of insulin, medical researcher Frederick Banting and research assistant Charles Best, thus putting Toronto on the world map of advanced science.

Figure 14: Ruth

Still, as vibrant as city life could be, for someone like Ruth, under-educated in the ways of commerce, the anxiety of setting off for parts unknown with an all-girl band was somewhat overwhelming. But no fear: the Keyfetzs, concerned that Ruth be protected in this new venture with Ina Ray Hutton, just happened to have a bright brother who was an up-and-coming lawyer. Murray Keyfetz never had a chance to refuse, given the insistence of his sisters that "poor Ruthie needs protection." He put together a contract that would ensure Ruth Lowe would not be taken advantage of out on the road.

And so, off sailed Ruthie as the newest Melodear in the land.

The connection with Murray would grow and become a lifeline later on.

Being on the road as a Melodear was a crazy existence: all the girls played poker between appearances and they all smoked... everyone smoked back then. But Ruthie sent money home regularly, and that was so important.

As for the band, Mickey shares this opinion: "Ina Ray wasn't a great musician. But she was a darn fine-looking gal, and really good on stage. She sure could dance."

Figure 15: Harold Cohen

Time moves on, and, eventually, Ruth meets a music publicist—a "song plugger" in the phraseology of the day—named Harold Cohen. His job was to work with music publishers and radio stations to get songs heard.

Ina Ray's band had hit Chicago where Ruth and her friend, Lil Huston, the Melodear's drummer, decided to head out on the town along with Lil's husband, an Illinois fight commissioner.

They set Ruthie up on a blind date with their friend, Harold Cohen, and off the four of them went. Who knew the stars were going to shine so brilliantly between the pretty pianist and the handsome publicist? Not long after, Harold proposed.

"He was a great guy," says Mickey. "Ruth brought Harold up to Toronto so my mother and I could meet him before the wedding. Tall man. Very good-looking man. Very nice man. I was really happy Ruthie had met someone like this. I even met his family: lovely people, made me feel very much at home."

Ruth had fallen big time for Harold, so much so that she decided to leave Ina Ray's band and spend more time with this man of her dreams, somebody who had come along at the right time in her life who she hoped would stabilize things, making her more safe and secure.

"The wedding took place at my grandfather's house on Baldwin Street in Toronto," Lynda Rapp, Murray Keyfetz's daughter, recalls. "They'd just come up from Chicago and Ruth didn't know any big shooters and neither she nor her fiancé had the kind of bucks to run a big wedding back then. So, my late father stepped up to the plate, as he had when he worked out that contract that kept Ruth protected on the road with the Melodears. And stepping up to the plate *also* meant offering himself up to be Harold Cohen's best man. And stepping up to the plate *also* meant providing the Keyfetz grand family home as the venue for the ceremony!"

With the pressure off for making a success of the wedding, both Ruth and Harold said their vows, enjoyed the occasion with family and friends, and looked forward to a blissful life together.

Post nuptials, the newly married Cohens returned to Chicago, ready to set out on the fine voyage of their new lives.

It was a time of innocent joy, with visions of future babies sparkling in their heads. Harold kept plugging songs and Ruth worked as a pianist with the publishers Bregman, Vocco, and Conn.

But then, tragedy met head-on with the vibrant young couple's very being, striking a clashing chord that would reverberate over a lifetime.

Not yet married a year, Harold had gone to the hospital for what was to be a routine operation.

The Fates had a different song to play.

"We had no inkling that he was ill, my mother and me," Mickey confesses. "And then, we get this phone call from Ruth saying he's dead. Kidney failure. It was just such a shock!"

Ruth was dumbstruck. Heartbroken. She had loved Harold deeply. But now, as a doleful young lady, she was suddenly alone. Anguished. Devastated.

We need to take a break here to reflect on the profound depth of despair Harold's death caused his pretty young wife. Of course, any bride would be shattered by her husband's sudden passing, coming as it did without warning. But for Ruth Lowe, the stakes were exceptional.

After all, she had grown up wanting—*needing*—love. Not that her family was estranged—not at all. But her father was focused on trying to make so many failed attempts at various businesses work that "family time" was not as high on his list as it should have been. Singing, dancing, and playing poker with the ladies was a form of relaxation that the gregarious, heavyset charmer enjoyed when away from the demands of being a poor butcher trying to put food on the table.

And then, one day, Sam was gone.

"I think he was deeply bothered that he wasn't a more dependable provider for the family," Mickey remembers.

And there was Pearl, of course, as Ruth's and Muriel's mother, trying somehow to carry on.

"My father had brought a great deal of stress and heartache to my mother's life," Mickey states sadly. "He never earned enough to support the family. Always off on the next big idea. My memories of my mother are clouded by recollections of years of struggle, unhappiness, and strain. And that was followed by her

Figure 16: Ruth

suffering from a serious heart condition. Both Ruth and I found her hard to be close to, really."

Living wasn't easy. After Sam's death, Pearl, Ruth, and Muriel had moved around often. Here they were: two pretty ingénues with the future beckoning, experiencing a life of day-to-day uncertainty through a bitter mother who'd all but given up, enduring faded memories of an absentee father who had become little more than a pale recollection. It was an upbringing that left Ruth wanting.

But there was more. Ruth had inherited her father's musical creativity. Perhaps because of that inventiveness—coupled with the classic, universal quest to find love and fulfillment that most of us feel—she had a need to connect, to share, to be a part of something larger. Her creative heart and soul called out for love, having lost her father and now coping with the somewhat cool, sad demeanor of her mother. The answer was to take tragedy and turn it into triumph, as only a creative young woman could do.

It's safe to say that Ruth didn't really experience any kind of meaningful closeness until she met Harold. Not that she was a "looking-for-love-in-all-the-wrong-places" kind of gal. She was too smart for that. Yet, there was a somewhat anguished need in her life that was unfulfilled.

And then: *bang*!: along comes this handsome, caring, doting man, Harold Cohen, who actually shared her love of the music business! What could be more perfect? He could finally bring love to Ruth in the way that had been absent for far too long. It was like a Hollywood scenario. At last—after so-near-yet-so-far experiences—Ruth discovers love in all its glory.

But then, it's rudely snatched from her, abruptly, with absolutely no advance warning!

The love of her life—finally actualizing the gap she had sought so desperately to fill—is ripped from her soul.

Her life is ruptured.

Love is nothing more than a sad prank, a one-liner destined to pull her into the depths of despair.

Figure 17: I'll Never Smile Again

"She was in a fog," Mickey explains. "Somehow, she had to clear up her affairs in Chicago. And then, she came back to Toronto, to our third-floor apartment, across from Christie Pitts Park. She moved in with me and our mother. And Ruthie would just sit, watching young couples strolling arm in arm in the park. She was very depressed. It was too great a tragedy for her to bear."

For tears would fill my eyes
My heart would realize
That our romance is through[12]

The days drew on. Yet, eventually, reality reasserted itself. Ruth awakened to the need to get out and loosen her thoughts of torment. She also had to keep the rent checks flowing and ensure food was in supply. So, she went to work at a local radio station, followed by stints at the Canadian Broadcasting Corporation (CBC).

"She had a very hard time," Mickey says. "Harold had been the first real love of her life. And this terrible thing happens. It was... It just tore her apart. She was trying to work, but..."

Mickey then reveals the birth of the song that would define her sister's life.

"I'll never forget it," she says. "Ruthie was just so sad. Trying to go to work, trying to get her life back on track, but just so very sad. And, one day, she says to me, 'Mickey, I just don't think I'll ever smile again.' And, you know, hearing her saying that just tore *my* heart out."

But, even in her grief, Ruth realized she'd stumbled onto a pretty sensational song title, if only by chance. That night, in June of 1939, she sat down to write it out. In fairly short order, the song that would define her life simply poured from her soul. The ballad "seemed to fill my head and guide my fingers as I picked it out on the piano," she'd recall later.

---

[12] I'll Never Smile Again, Words and Music by Ruth Lowe, Copyright © 1939 UNIVERSAL MUSIC CORP., Copyright Renewed, All Rights Reserved, Used by Permission, Reprinted by Permission of Hal Leonard LLC.

I'll Never Smile Again
Until I smile at you
I'll never laugh again
What good would it do...[13]

Even though it was born of shattering personal pain, Miss Lowe was enough of a realist to accept the value of universalizing her situation, elevating it from a dirge to something more all-embracing, *comme ça*:

For tears would fill my eyes
My heart would realize
That our romance is through...[14]

Mickey is asked if she was the first person to ever hear the song. "Before anyone else?" she thinks back. "Well, yes, I guess I was the first. But you know, it was nice and everything..." She looks around, lowering her voice almost to a conspirator's whisper, "but I never thought it would become the big hit it did. Really, it just seemed like another song, you know. Who knew it would take off the way it did?"

Still, Mickey is not unimpressed by the success her sister's talent achieved. "The mournful tune and lyrics really spoke to people," she says. "After all, World War II was casting its terrible shadow across the globe, and here comes this song like something out of a dream."

"It was hugely important and a huge hit," comments Sinatra biographer James Kaplan. "The timing was right: what made Sinatra a superstar was World War II. When 'I'll Never Smile Again' hit, it was a very rough year. The ballads of yearning that

---

[13] I'll Never Smile Again, Words and Music by Ruth Lowe, Copyright © 1939 UNIVERSAL MUSIC CORP., Copyright Renewed, All Rights Reserved, Used by Permission, Reprinted by Permission of Hal Leonard LLC.
[14] I'll Never Smile Again, Words and Music by Ruth Lowe, Copyright © 1939 UNIVERSAL MUSIC CORP., Copyright Renewed, All Rights Reserved, Used by Permission, Reprinted by Permission of Hal Leonard LLC.

Sinatra sang during this time jet-propelled his career. Even though he was detested overseas by the fighting men who thought he was back at home misbehaving with their wives, there's no question that 'I'll Never Smile Again' was the greatest of those ballads of yearning. It was the peak of Sinatra's early career, the peak of his fame, and it was all built around that song."

Let's take a brief detour here to explore just how Ruth was able to take her extreme grief and turn it to her advantage. Our tour guide is Yvonne Heath, author of *"Love Your Life To Death."* She's a former nurse who's realized that our death-phobic society all too often avoids talking about—and planning for—death.

"Grief is our reaction to a loss," she explains. "It's the sadness of a change in your life that you don't want or haven't anticipated. Now, if you are a creative person, such as Ruth Lowe was, then you can use that creativity to work your way through your grief. Catharsis allows whatever is bubbling up inside of you to be expressed, helps you rid yourself of the grief of that feeling. Ritual can be helpful in dealing with grief too. So, I think it was part of Ruth's healing because she was already very musical." As an example, Yvonne cites many paintings that have been created by artists dealing with grief.

"It's an amazing gift to the world that Ruth left," she adds. "A beautiful legacy. Anybody who's experienced such a tragedy, if you can create something wonderful from it by helping other people deal with similar trauma and grief, then, I think, that's extraordinary. I'm sure it was part of Ruth's own healing, but it helped a lot of people deal with their special loss too."

Beyond creativity, however, there was a certain amount of providence at play here, aiding the trajectory of the tune.

First off, with Ruth working at the CBC, she had come into contact with Canadian musician Percy Faith, a gentleman who would go on to fame in the U.S. and worldwide. He had a radio program back then called "Music By Faith."

"So many people think Ruth was American," Mickey says. "And they assume Mr. Faith was American too. He made his name there later on, of course, as the man who really fashioned 'easy listening' music into such popularity. But he was born and raised in Toronto. Did you know he was Jewish too?"

Research bears out that Percy Faith was one of eight children born to Abraham Faith and Minnie Rottenberg. He grew up in Toronto's Jewish pushcart district, which later became Kensington Market. As a child, Percy played violin and piano, but suffered through a life changing fire that severely burned his hands. He could not know it then, but this accident would pave the way for new dimensions in music.

"Percy was at home practising," writes Alfred Holden in his award-winning essay on the musician published in *Taddle Creek Magazine*.

> *The only other family member around was his sister Gertrude, who was three. He heard her scream. Rushing upstairs he found her aflame. She had been playing with matches. "I took her clothes off while it was burning," he remembered, "and it burnt my hands." Both kids would mend, but Faith, then eighteen, changed direction. Unable to play the piano for nine months, "I put a pencil in the bandages in my hand," he said, "and I started to study composition. When I found that, then I knew what I wanted to do." Reflecting on the incident later in life, Percy Faith said, "They say something good comes out of everything bad. It made a new life for me.*[15]

---

[15] *Taddle Creek*, "The Streamlined Man," Alfred Holden, 2000, Christmas (4), see https://www.taddlecreekmag.com/the-streamlined-man.

No longer able to pursue playing instruments, the inventive young man turned to conducting orchestras, soon becoming a staple of the CBC's live music programs. And then "Music By Faith" was picked up by the Mutual Broadcasting System in the U.S., where, oddly, it won the ear and approval of gossip columnist Walter Winchell, not given to compliments and not fond of things foreign. "Don't miss Percy Faith's orchestra from Toronto," Winchell wrote. "Full of strings and melody—best since Paul Whiteman's vogue." Eager praise indeed.

"So here we have two people whose lives had taken unexpected turns, both working at the CBC," Mickey explains. "Ruth Lowe and Percy Faith. And Ruthie had a friend, Vida Guthrie: she was Percy's musical arranger. Sensing that her song might have some demand, Ruth decided to take it to Vida, asking if she'd play it for the boss."

Indeed, Percy Faith heard "I'll Never Smile Again" and fell in love with the song. "He asked Ruth if he could record it as well as perform it on the radio," Mickey says.

And here's where the next bit of magic happened. With Percy Faith's enthusiasm, and that of others who heard the tune and extolled its virtues, young Ruth began wondering if her sad lament had legs. And having legs in those days meant being picked up by a band like Tommy Dorsey's. Fortunately, she now had a swell recording of her song, delivered expressly to her on a disk by Percy Faith.

So, how do we get from Faith to Dorsey?

"Ahhh, that's easy," explains Mickey. "You see, Ina Ray Hutton's sister, June, sang with the Pied Pipers, Dorsey's singing group. Turns out June was dating Dorsey's guitar player. All of the pieces started coming together, do you see?"

And so, it was that 1939 saw Tommy Dorsey and his orchestra due in Toronto to play at the Canadian National Exhibition. Ruth connects with June when she hits town and sets up a meeting with the singer's boyfriend. She plays the record for him: he reacts positively and suggests they play it for the boss.

Dorsey himself is staying at the Royal York Hotel. And when the guitar player drops by his room suggesting he just might want to listen to an intriguing record, TD agrees.

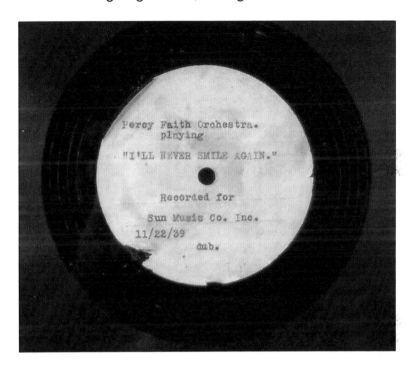

Figure 18: Percy Faith recording: I'll Never Smile Again

Now, typically, someone like Dorsey is handed lots of potential hit tunes for his consideration. And they are usually on paper, either concepts scratched out on a napkin or shirt cardboard, right up to more professional sheet music, this being the printed form of notation using symbols to indicate pitches and rhythms of a song or musical piece. But this time, it's different: the musician has Ruth Lowe's record! An actual recording of her song that she hopes Dorsey will admire. And not just any record. This one features the entire CBC orchestra—a lavish aggregation of woodwinds, strings, brass, and percussion, conducted by Percy Faith! This alone makes her submission stand out. So much so that when Mr. Dorsey hears the song, he immediately wants to hire Mr. Faith to arrange for him. For his part, Percy's not ready to make that big migration south. Not yet. His chance will come soon enough when, in 1945, he becomes a naturalized U.S. citizen and begins popularizing the "easy listening" music format, refining orchestration techniques, and adding large string sections to diminish the domination of brass.

Meanwhile, as they say, the rest is history. Dorsey loves the song and is ready to launch it into the stratosphere.

Mind you, there are theories about that. The popularity of "I'll Never Smile Again" was helped along by the "fact" that Ruth Lowe was an American whose poor flyboy husband was killed in action over Europe. Even Sinatra intoned that on a broadcast. But, when you recall that this is 1940 and the U.S. is still a year away from even entering World War II, how could that be? Still, why crowd a good story with truth? In a broader sense, Ruth's ballad, born from her own sad loss, managed to catch the mood of Americans—and then the world—reflecting the delicate nature of all wartime romance.

Figure 19: Ruth and Tommy Dorsey

Rob Fogle, Toronto-based host of the long-running weekly radio series *Some Experiences In Jazz*, adds this:

My dad told me he had driven Ruth to CBC to deliver her song to Percy Faith. He knew her through Hadassah. Skip ahead 35 years. Sinatra was making his trip to Toronto to appear at Maple Leaf Gardens in 1975—By the way, I have the largest collection of Sinatra stuff of anyone in the city, including 6-700 CDs. Anyway, Ruth goes backstage and spends a fair amount of time with Frank. And all her girlfriends are dying with curiosity afterwards: 'What did you talk about? What did you talk about?' And Ruth says simply, 'Our grandchildren!' That was how it went.

I was in the flower business back then, and Ruth used to rush in and buy flowers from me. And she didn't talk about the song, but she'd go on and on about Hadassah. She was very active: a hard worker.

You know, I'm always amazed at what 'I'll Never Smile Again' did for Sinatra. I mean, you've got the Pied Pipers in there in a big way— Sinatra's only part of it. No question the guy was destined for greatness, but I'm surprised it wasn't a song like 'Polka Dots and Moonbeams' that skyrocketed him forward. And I have to tell you, that first version of Ruth's song—Dorsey's version—it never really knocked me off my feet. But Frank's later version, the one with Gordon Jenkins: now, that's the one![16]

---

[16] Rob Fogle interview with Peter Jennings

Of course, Mr. Dorsey and Mr. Sinatra were not alone in recognizing the beauty of "I'll Never Smile Again." The song would go on to be covered through 150 versions, including everyone from the great Fats Waller, to England's Ted Heath, to Billie Holiday's haunting version (among the last of her recorded works in which she laid down an evocative track, perhaps aided by the fact she was in such poor health from years of substance abuse that a nurse sometimes had to help keep her propped up on a high stool as she sang Ruth's song), to Tal Bachman (son of the Guess Who's Randy Bachman), to...

Clearly, we're talking a song that has stood the test of time.

Back to Muriel Cohen.

"Mickey, how did you feel when you first heard the song played on the radio?" she's asked. "Would you stop people and say, 'That's my sister's song'?"

"I *still* do!" she laughs with pride. "Anytime I hear it, I'll announce to whoever I'm with, 'My sister Ruth wrote that song!' I'm very proud of my sister. The fact that she hit it so big was very impressive. She always had a terrific personality. She was very outgoing. And she was very good to me. She was a very good sister. She used to even buy clothes for me.

"Of course, Ruth is with me every day," Mickey confesses. "Visibly, you know... Look at that needlepoint hanging on the wall. Strange that for someone as busy and sophisticated as she was, Ruthie loved doing handiwork. She made blankets and pillows, all sorts of things. She had a real knack for it."

Sure. But the stronger knack was in crafting songs. Writing this one in particular—an anguished ballad that Ruth could not have known at the time was destined to become such an absolute worldwide musical phenomenon—offered her a much-needed release from the grip of death. It was as though the very act of penning the lyrics, coupled with inscribing a simple yet beguiling melody, formed a kind of get-out-of-jail-free card for her, releasing Ruth from the forbidden ground that had held her hostage, standing in the path of her future, preventing her from moving ahead with her life. Here was an Open Sesame—a virtual free pass—to a land of opportunity few people would ever experience.

Ruth Lowe was not only about to be released, she was soon to set sail on such an astonishing adventure that even her wildest imagination could never conceive it.

Chapter Seven

Celebrity!

"Dorsey was a great marketer," explains James Kaplan. "Once he saw how 'I'll Never Smile Again' was taking off, with sales of records and sheet music, he brought Ruth to New York City and made sure her story became known."

Ruth Lowe was famous, no doubt about it. And following the release of "I'll Never Smile Again," her life changed dramatically. People wanted to know all about the young lass who had written this wonderful song and the story behind its creation. She made a number of public appearances and quickly rose to fame in the music industry. Soon, she was being interviewed by newspaper and magazine columnists, she was featured on radio shows and even began making public appearances wherever people wanted to see the girl who'd written "the song." One such appearance saw her being part of comedian Red Skelton's vaudeville show. And she had a less than stellar moment when she tripped over the bolted down shoes used by a comedian to "lean over" into the audience: Ruthie ended up in the lap of someone in the first row, laughing her head off.

Figure 20: Ruth

By now, Miss Lowe was getting huge amounts of fan mail to add to her acclaim. Everyone wanted her picture. It was quickly getting to the point where she couldn't handle all the hoopla on her own.

"So, she calls up to Toronto from New York," Mickey says.

"And she pleads with me, 'I need you to come down here. Right away. You'll be my secretary.'"

Figure 21: From Ruth's scrapbook

Mickey pauses, looks out the window, recalling the thrill of the times.

"Now I ask you, who's going to say no to that?"

The Lowe sisters took up residence at the Astor Hotel in Times Square. It was right across the street from where Frank Sinatra was appearing at the Paramount Theatre with the Pied Pipers.

"We'd see and meet many of the great stars who came to play the Paramount," says Mickey. "But Sinatra was special. You know, he was a proud New Jersey boy who would often refer to his hometown of Hoboken, and it struck me then that he was one whose success seemed to come simply because he was so good at what he did. Even to hear his songs today, especially one of Ruth's songs, I still get teary eyed."

After one of his shows, Sinatra came back to their room.

"Ruthie asked him to say hi to me," Mickey recalls. "Well, I just about died."

Having been introduced to the thrilling world of celebrities and talented artists who she'd grown up only dreaming about, Mickey now joined Ruth in her outings to the famed Tin Pan Alley offices of music publishers where she'd play the new tunes she'd written.

And the entrepreneur in Ruth Lowe—perhaps passed on by the spirit of her father, although with more adherence to success—got to work capitalizing on her *éclat*. She and Sair Lee soon developed a weekly radio show for NBC where the two would play the songs of the day, singing and kibitzing throughout. They were known as "The Shadows" and Tom Sandler has a recording of one of their shows that begins, "Howdy neighbour, you're listening to The Blue Network, NBC."

"I used to get such a kick out of Sair's name," Tom recalls. "Sair Lee. Just like a Sara Lee banana cake, one of my faves to this day! Oh, by the way, before I forget, mom made a killer banana cream pie!"

Ruth also wrote "The Lowe Down," a jazz column read widely in New York and elsewhere. And to fill in her quiet hours (not!), she happened to manage the Murray Room, a New York jazz night club.

And you wonder why she needed her sister's help!

"Ruth even got me a job at a music store in New York," Mickey says." And she brought our mother down to live with us. Now I have to say, for our mother, it was trying. She had no friends or family in that great big city. But for me? A fabulous time in my life! And Ruthie, no matter how different our lives were or wherever her success took her, she was always there for me. A strong, giving sister, so full of life."

Propelled by her remarkable talent and spurred on by the tune that was becoming so beloved, Ruth Lowe had entered a glamorous world of famous stages and celebrated entertainers. Her acquaintances ranged from Sinatra and Dorsey, to Duke Ellington, to Sammy Cahn, to Ed Sullivan, to Henny Youngman, to Milton Berle, to Bob Hope, to Danny Kaye, to Vic Damone, to Buddy Rich, to Al Jolson, to... and on and on. She even introduced fellow Canadian, Jack Duffy, to Tommy Dorsey and he ended up singing with TD for a while. The fact that Duffy bore a slight resemblance to Sinatra didn't hurt.

And then, there was "The Happy Gang," a hugely popular Canadian Broadcasting Corp. lunchtime variety radio show that ran from 1937 to

Figure 22 Ruth with Bob Hope

1959 with about two million listeners a day. A mention there, on the CBC, could pay off big time, and with the Gang supporting Ruth and her song, this only added to her zest.

Most importantly, Ruth Lowe was gaining a reputation as one of the architects of the American Ballad.

Never one to sit still for long, Ruthie itched to write more songs. Sometimes on her own, more than often collaborating with the gang from the Brill building, she wrote "Too Beautiful to Last" with Marty Symes, created for the 1941 MGM film *Ziegfeld Girl* with James Stewart and Judy Garland. And "My First Love," which she penned with Mack David. And "My Love Came Back to Me" with George Fragos, famous for his hit "I Hear A Rhapsody," and several others. In fact, in September 1940, when Dorsey and his orchestra returned to Toronto for another Canadian National Exhibition performance, he not only played "I'll Never Smile Again" but, caught up with the enthusiastic reception of Ruth Lowe returning to her hometown for this engagement, he featured "My Next Romance" and "Funny Little Pedro," two of her new songs.

Now, being as active as she was, Ruth wasn't terribly surprised one day in 1943 when she got a phone call from Sinatra. What ensued was a conversation like this...

"Hey, doll, I need you to write me a song."

"A song, Frankie?" Ruth questions. "What kind of song?"

"Gonna be my theme song," Sinatra explains with pride. You can practically see him puffing out his chest. After all, by now, he's left the Dorsey organization and struck out on his own as a solo performer. "I hope you fall on your ass" is the send-off he gets from Mr. Dorsey, none too happy to see his meal ticket vanishing.

"CBS is giving me a radio show," Sinatra explains to Ruth, "I need a tune I can be known for. You know Ruthie, something I can sing at the beginning or end of each show that will be my signature tune. Got it?"

"OK, Frankie. Now, what are you thinking of for the mood?"

"The mood? Hmmm. The mood. Well, I'm thinking it's something that will be pretty...I dunno...something about...maybe...maybe sweet dreams? The show's at night, so you know, Ruthie...like maybe I sing this at the end of each show and it's like you'd say 'Sweet dreams" to someone as they fall off to sleep. But I don't know, Ruth...you'll come up with something."

"OK Frankie. Leave this with me. I'll play around with it and get back to you with some ideas. When do you need this for?"

"Um... See, that's the problem."

"The problem?"

"Yeah. See, we need it for tomorrow."

"What!?"

"Yeah. Sorry 'bout that. They just laid this on me, and the first show's tomorrow night."

"Frankie! I... ... mean...tomorrow night! I can't..."

"Ruthie, you told me you wrote 'I'll Never Smile Again' in one evening. You can do this. You're so *good* at this."

"But, Frank, that was totally different. I mean..."

"Look, I gotta go. So many things we need to work on for this show. There's just no time. Anyway, you'll nail this, I just know you will. Call me tomorrow morning. OK, Ruthie?"

"Yeah. Sure Frankie. Sure. I'll call you tomorrow..."

Click.

Well, truth be told, Ruth *had* created her signature tune "I'll Never Smile Again" in an evening. But, as she'd tried to explain to the irrepressible Sinatra, that was different. That was a song that poured from her heart because of anguish. A song that had been building within her for months and months and finally needed to break through the emotional dam and get out.

But now, a theme song for the hottest singer in the land? A signature tune that would be heard by millions of people? Every week? For...like...forever?

And it had to be composed in less than 24 hours?

Impossible.

Unless...

Following in the trail of headliners, like Irving Berlin and Cole Porter, who famously wrote both the lyrics and the music when most Tin Pan Alley tunesmiths created songs in duos, Ruth had created the melody and words for "I'll Never Smile Again" on her own. She'd even said to an interviewer, "George and Ira Gershwin, Rodgers and Hart, Johnny Mercer and Harold Arlen, yes, I'm aware that many tunes have been created by song writing duos. And I understand that, especially when you're turning out a bunch of songs for the next Broadway show or Hollywood movie. But that's not me. I'm not a song writing machine and don't want to be. I'm just a girl who writes songs when I feel like it. When I'm inspired to do so. And that's something I can do on my own."

But with the clock ticking, it's definitely time for Plan B.

So, Ruth places a call to two song writing buddies, Paul Mann and Stephan Weiss. Now, these lads have been collaborating on creating lovely lilts like "They Say" and "Angel in Disguise" as well as novelty tunes such as "The Woodchuck Song" (featuring the ebullient lyric, "How much wood would a woodchuck chuck if a woodchuck could chuck wood?").

"You guys got a tune lying around you're not doing anything with?" Ruth asks on the phone.

There is laugher. "Hey Ruthie, good to hear from you. What kind of a question is that? Whadyamean do we have a tune lying around?"

Ruth explains the predicament she's facing. She knows that these two guys are always batting out melodies, sometimes adding lyrics and trying to peddle new tunes. And sometimes, when the song doesn't quite click, the tune or the lyrics go on the shelf, awaiting inspiration for a future date.

Ruth just hopes today's shelf might feature a lovely tune looking for words. You know, one that would do as a theme song for the most in-demand vocalist in the country. You know, by tomorrow.

"24 hours!" They respond with laughter after hearing her story. "You're kidding, right? Frankie Sinatra needs his theme song by tomorrow!?"

But Ruth tells them it's no joke.

And as chance would have it, turns out the boys *do* have a tune they've been playing with. Not fully finished, mind you, but part way there.

"My father was a fabulous piano player," says Lindy Kahn, daughter of the late Paul Mann who passed away in 1983. Lindy, an educational consultant, sits in the stylish home in Houston, Texas that she shares with her husband, Sanford, an attorney.

"People don't know that about him," she continues. "I mean, his reputation is as a song writer and, yes, he was born in Vienna and worked as a film composer in Berlin before coming to the U.S. in 1938. But he *loved* playing the piano. He played with flair and passion. He played in the Catskills and my mother, Yvonne— her mother was an opera singer, you know—she sang with him on stage."

"My dad felt that rock and roll really killed composing good music," Lindy continues. "He had bitterness about that, about not being able to continue composing good songs that the world seemed not to need anymore. It took away his motivation. He actually wanted to be a conductor. But he had to put food on the table for my mother and me and my brother, so he stopped writing songs and went back to his first love, playing the piano in clubs and restaurants. In fact, I have beautiful memories of him playing every year on my birthday. It was magical!"

"And, you know, just like Ruth Lowe, Dad hung out with Sammy Cahn and Jimmy Van Heusen and all the famous songwriters, and eventually some of these guys asked him to go to Hollywood and work for Warner Brothers. But Paul Mann was not a risk taker. He chose to stay home with my mom and my brother and me and play the piano."

Lindy pauses and looks off. "It's just too bad you didn't contact me a few months ago when Mom was still alive. She could have told you so much."

Meanwhile, the clock is ticking, and Ruth Lowe needs a song. A big song.

Paul moves to the piano while Stephan holds the phone over the soundboard. He bangs out the gist of a tune, one they've been playing around with. When done, he feels the need to make excuses.

"I mean, Ruth, it's not finished. But I don't know, I think there could be something there..."

"I like it!" Ruth gushes, feeling somewhat pleased with herself that she's made the right call. "You know what, guys, I've got some words I've been throwing around for a song," she tells them. "Haven't really finished anything. But they might work with that melody..."

The three of them agree that with the partially finished tune the boys have at hand, and with Ruth's lyrics part way there, they might just have a fighting chance to pull a rabbit from the hat.

A sleepless night transpires.

And by the crack of dawn, Ruth Lowe's singing...

> *Put your dreams away for another day*[17]
> *And I will take their place in your heart.*

---

[17] Put Your Dreams Away, words and music by Paul Mann, Stephen Weiss and Ruth Lowe, Copyright © (Renewed) Chappell & Co., Inc. and Barton Music Corp., all rights outside of the US Controlled by Chappell & Co., Inc., all rights reserved, used by permission of Alfred Music, also
Put Your Dreams Away (For Another Day), words by Ruth Lowe, Music by Stephan Weiss and Paul Mann, Copyright © 1942, 1943 by Chappell & Co and BMG Firefly, Copyright Renewed, All Rights for BMG Firefly Administered by BMG Rights Management (US) LLC, All Right Reserved, Used by Permission, Reprinted by Permission of Hal Leonard LLC.

Wishing on a star never got you far
And so, it's time to make a new start.

It's a slow-tempo, romantic ballad with Ruth's dream-like lyrics reminding listeners they'll find love wherever it's offered.

Before noon, they've wrapped it up. She places a call to Sinatra.

"Frankie, listen to this," Ruth says earnestly as she places the phone on the piano and begins to play and sing the song that will serve as his signature tune for 25 years. The ballad that will be the last song played at his funeral in 1998.

She finishes and waits breathlessly for the verdict.

"Ruthie..." Sinatra intones.

"Yes Frank," she says. *He hates it*, she thinks.

"I *love* it. Play it again. It's great. I knew you'd come through."

The smile overtaking her nervous face signals to the boys: *We did it!*

And for the *second* time in her short life, Ruth Lowe has joined her star to that of the biggest talent in the land.

"I'll never forget watching our black and white TV in the 1950s," says Lindy Kahn. "When Frank threw that raincoat over his shoulder and walked off singing "Put Your Dreams Away" at the end of the show, well, I sure knew this was an important moment in our household."

Sinatra's keen sense of music knew it too. "Dear old theme song," he intones on

Figure 23: Put Your Dreams Away

his Grammy-winning album, *Sinatra: A Man and His Music*, "I love you, old buddy." He later praises the song for having come a long way with him—"All the way from nowhere to somewhere."

That "somewhere," by the way, includes Sinatra singing "Put Your Dreams Away" on his radio and television shows, often in concert, and in a number of different versions he recorded for albums. That somewhere also being an opportunity for Barry Manilow to sing the tune on his Grammy-nominated album, *Manilow Sings Sinatra*, and numerous cover versions recorded by the likes of Perry Como, The Hi-Lo's, cornetist Bobby Hackett, The Nelson Riddle Orchestra, the Ray Charles Singers, The Singers Unlimited, Eileen Farrell in an arrangement by Robert Farnon, Ranee Lee, John McDermott, Gisele MacKenzie, and many others. And that "somewhere" also saw "Put Your Dreams Away" used in Stanley Kubrick's film *Lolita*, and in the movie *Inside Moves* (1980).

"I have to tell you, it's my favorite of all the songs mom wrote," Tom Sandler says. "I just love the positive, evocative feeling of those words."

In fact, more than 75 years after its first appearance, Ruth Lowe's lovely ballad still has lasting appeal, surely the mark of a distinguished ditty that once again took the world by storm.

Chapter Eight

Anatomy of a Song

Famed song lyricist Sammy Cahn always had a swell answer when asked, "What comes first, the words or the music?"

"The phone call!" he would intone dryly.

Still, in all seriousness, it is worth noting that Mr. Cahn regularly worked with musicians when composing songs. He knew his limits.

So too, Richard Rodgers and Lorenz Hart. And later Rodgers and Oscar Hammerstein. And George and Ira Gershwin. And Jerome Kern and almost anyone. And Harold Arlen with many wordsmiths, like Yip Harburg and Johnny Mercer.

With the notable exceptions of Cole Porter and Irving Berlin, most contributors to the Great American Songbook made their entries as duos. How much better to focus on one skill than two?

Ruth Lowe failed to learn this lesson. In fact, when she sat down to let "I'll Never Smile Again" flow out of her heart, it never occurred to her to team up with anyone else.

It was *her* song. *Her* life. *Her* emotion.

Pretty amazing when you think about it.

Not only do we have a *woman* writing a chart-busting song (hmmmm—let's see—in 1940, we have Dorothy Fields and... hmmmm), but she's knocking both the tune *and* the story right out of the park!

So, considering that, and the fact that this wonderfully sad anthem managed to leap head-over-heels above the fray to outclass every happy-go-lucky competitive tune of the time, at this point in our story, it's worth considering how "I'll Never Smile Again" had such staying power.

Turning to the experts seems like a reasonable strategy.

For instance, Bernard John Taupin. He thinks he may just have an answer...

Bernie Taupin

*Definitely in the top 50 of great American
songs. It's a phenomenal song!*

As the lyricist to Sir Elton John's tunes, now celebrating a collaboration between the two of them that transcends 50 years together—one of the most successful song writing partnerships in musical history—Bernie Taupin's ready to share a secret: "I have far more appreciation for the music of the past generations than I do of my own," he says, *sotto vocce*.

Can this be? The guy who writes words for Elton's hits doesn't really dig rock 'n roll? The author of "Your Song," "Saturday Night's Alright for Fighting," and "Goodbye Yellow Brick Road"? The fact is, he's more at home grooving to a Louis Armstrong lick or a Lionel Hampton riff or Dean Martin's crooning than he is hearing a Kanye West screed. Who knew?

"Yeah, yeah. I mean, of course, I know who Kanye West is," Bernie says. "Have I ever heard one of his songs? I don't think so. I mean, I guess I could have and not known about it.

"But don't get me wrong," he clarifies as he stretches out on the leather couch in the art studio that sits amidst 28 acres of his horse ranch in the Santa Ynez Valley, California. "It's just, I don't really care for pop music. All I ever listen to is jazz and blues. I've always gravitated to music from the past. Don't agree with my friend, John Lennon, who said, 'Before Elvis, there was nothing.' Well, no lack of respect for John, but I believe before Elvis there was everything. And after Elvis there was a lot less!"

Bernie also confesses, "I spend very little of my time writing songs anymore. I spend all my time in my studio, painting." The inveterate rancher adds, "Frankly, I'd rather rope a horse than write a song."

As for "I'll Never Smile Again" and how it transcended the up-tempo challengers, he offers this: "It was a dangerous move to make with that song, no question. And a brave move to make as well. Because there was so much other cute stuff going on. But let me tell you why the song broke through—I mean, apart from the fact that it's such a wonderful song. Two words: Frank Sinatra. He was the only person who could have done that song. He knew he could have the bobby-soxers hysterically screaming one minute and crying the next. And this was the song to do it! Without Sinatra, the song would never have charted as well. Ruth Lowe probably achieved more by being bold enough to write something that wasn't palatable to audiences of that era. They wanted dance music. But it goes back to Sinatra: only he could calm those maniacal fans. They could be screaming one second and hanging on to every word the next, because of his persona. He's the only person who could have done that song at that time. And 'I'll Never Smile Again' was the song to do it."

Then, Bernie adds this intriguing thought about the subject matter of the song.

"Bear in mind, for myself, the songs that have a bleaker outlook are far more satisfying to write than ones that are positive. Songs that are of a darker nature just bring out more of the artist in you than writing a frothy up-tempo pop number. It's far more interesting to investigate the seamier side of things, the underbelly of life, the heartbreak. Heartbreak is more easily mined than the happy side of romance. And for Ruth, it was that: a real release valve. She had the God-given gift to be able to put her feelings into that song. And she knew it. And when you write something so great as that, you don't go back and try to improve on it. You can over-think things. She didn't."

And then he adds, "By the way, I don't think of myself as a lyricist. It's such a strange word... I'm a storyteller. And so was Ruth."

And as for where the tune ranks? "Definitely in the top 50 of great American songs," Bernie Taupin enthuses. "It's a phenomenal song. And when you consider the vast amount of incredible music and incredible compositions and thousands of incredible songs that make up the Great American Songbook, I think this is giving it a really good pat on the back, ranking it like that. It has such a wonderful place in American musical history. And the fact that it was the launching pad for Sinatra didn't hurt."

Taupin stops to consider another point. He looks around the detached guesthouse/studio originally designed as an indoor handball court. Later, it was transformed to a recording studio where multiple albums were cut. Today, it functions as an art studio with a gym and an upstairs office with a bathroom.

"You know what," he says, having gathered his thoughts. "Here's something I find really interesting about Ruth Lowe's two most significant songs with Sinatra. One started his career and the other ended it. I mean, 'Put Your Dreams Away' was the last song played at his funeral. Talk about bookending his life! For that alone, Ruth Lowe should be immortalized!"

Bernie is asked what specifically he likes about "I'll Never Smile Again." His response is crowded with enthusiasm—and remember we're talking to one of the top tunesmiths to ever write a song, anytime, anywhere. "You have to think about where it comes from," he says. "The emotional impact of the song from her perspective. It's directly from the heart. You know, when a lot of us write a song—and believe me, I'm not putting myself in her league at all—the one thing we have is the ability to put it down as a song. It's a great attribute to be able to do that as a songwriter. But, with Ruth, it was an absolute exhalation of despair and sadness. It comes across in the song. And the fact that she was able to get the greatest voice of the 20th century to sing it was her ace in the hole. Because nobody understood and respected songwriters and lyricists the way Sinatra did. That was why he was as great as he was."

Bernie Taupin is not done expressing his fervour—and, at that, he's known as something of a curmudgeon who eschews speaking to the media. Certainly, he has given few newspaper interviews to provide clues about the person behind the music. "The more people I meet, the more I like my dogs," he explains. But his wife, Heather, has importuned, knowing of his love for the

Great American Songbook, and suddenly, he's keen to engage in the subject of Ruth Lowe's famous song.

"Dorsey saw the potential in the song, no question" Bernie says, rising to the occasion. "And it was kismet: that voice, that song, those words. They all belonged together. No one could give it the kind of interpretation he did. It was phenomenal. Even when Sinatra was that young."

Alan Bergman

> *"Great" is over-used. So, I'll say it's a good*
> *song: it did what it set out to do. Very well.*

Now, there are some other celebrated songwriters who have opinions about this song and how and why it hit so hard. People like Alan Bergman. Along with his wife Marilyn, this song writing duo has won Academy Awards and Grammys for their tunes, and they've been inducted into the Songwriters Hall of Fame. They can also claim that many of their songs have been recorded by the likes of Barbra Streisand and Sinatra himself.

Alan's just ventured in from his Californian garden where he's been picking oranges in the sun. "Always happy to take a break to talk about great songs," he says.

Having written both words and music in his time, Alan Bergman has respect for people who can do both. People like Ruth Lowe. "My ability to write music was not as good as the people who can do it really well," he explains. "Stick to what you're good at. For me, that's lyrics."

As for "I'll Never Smile Again," he's asked if he considers this standard to be a great song. "'Great' is so over-used," he says. "So, I'll say it's a good song: it did what it set out to do. And it did it very well."

When asked if he has ever written a song out of the kind of desperation Ruth felt, he responds, "Desperation? No. But you know, Marilyn and I have been writing in a dramatic way for a long time, dramatic situations in life. Dealing with anger—if that's what is called for—it can be effective. 'The Trouble With Hello is Goodbye,' which we wrote with Dave Grusin, deals with the end of a love affair. That's sad. But desperation? No."

And as for what makes a song like "I'll Never Smile Again" a chart topper?

"Good melody and a lyric that says something," he intones. "Songs that are entirely original, music in the case of standards, usually the melody and the lyric receive an amount of prominence. The melody is really the thing that is memorable. For a song to have character is where, at a certain point, you hear the melody, but you think of the lyric. The Gershwins, Porter, Berlin, Harold Arlen, their music could be played in any tempo, and it's always attractive. Lyrics that are so wonderful that the song becomes a standard."

Marilyn and Alan have been the go-to songwriters for Barbra Streisand for many years. And so, it's natural to ask why she never got around to recording "I'll Never Smile Again."

"You know, that's a good question," Alan says. "I don't know. She's the best in the world. But of the performers today, who could really nail that song, it would be Lady GaGa. She's very gifted. She's one of the few young people who know how to sing these songs. A lot of them try, but they don't make it, you know. But she knows. She seems to have that inner sense."

Which seems like a good entree to inquire who's writing songs today that he admires.

"Stephen Sondheim," is the quick reply. "No one writes songs like him. Just wonderful, the lyrics are... he's the best: the bar is way up there."

And how about you, Alan, are you and Marilyn still writing songs?

"Absolutely, we're writing a musical for the stage and an animated movie at the same time."

Given that Mr. Bergman is 90 years of age at the time of this discussion, it's suggested to him that this is pretty impressive.

"Hey, it's not exactly heavy lifting. A couple of pencils. And it's too much fun!! When you do something you love, and you write with somebody you love, it's great, right? It's a great life!"

Sir Tim Rice

It's a lovely song. It's a great song.

Speaking of a great life, let's head to England and check in with a certain Sir Timothy Miles Bindon Rice, winner of an Oscar, a Grammy, Golden Globe Award, Tony Award... He's best known for his collaborations with Andrew Lloyd Webber, with whom he's written lyrics for "Joseph and the Amazing Technicolor Dreamcoat," "Jesus Christ Superstar," and "Evita." And for his work for Walt Disney Studios with Alan Menken ("Aladdin," "Beauty and the Beast," "King David"), and Elton John ("The Lion King," "Aida," "The Road to El Dorado").

"Please call me Tim," he says as we initiate our discussion about Ruth Lowe's masterpiece. "And about those awards, of course, I'm always happy to be nominated. But one should never take them too seriously. There's lots of luck involved. And it's not just you: there are other aspects, including your co-writer."

So, what does one of the 20th and 21st century's most celebrated songwriters think of Ruth Lowe's song?

"'I'll Never Smile Again' is a great song," he says. "It's a lovely song. And the one that got Frank Sinatra to be so big. His voice is so perfect for that song. It's a truly lovely song. And I know she was a musician, but she'd never written a hit before. 'Put Your Dreams Away' is a lovely song as well. Very, very talented lady."

When asked about Ruth's ability to write music as well as lyrics, he confesses to having tried his hand with that duality in the past.

"Only simple stuff," he laughs. "I've actually had a few tunes recorded, but they've only been B-sides, you know. If you can do both, it's a rare ability. Like Ruth. But, sometimes, I'm glad that I really only do one thing because when I work with Andrew or

Elton, for instance, there's a real division of labor. You know, each of us can be critical, objective, and that can make for a better overall song. And you simply don't have that if you're on your own. Not that this doesn't stop people like Ruth or like Cole Porter from writing brilliant stuff. But I'll hear a tune with a really crappy lyric, and I'll think that, you know, it could have been better if it had a different lyric—let's put it that way."

Sir Tim's got a great sense of humor. When asked, in consideration of Ruth's desperation in writing her landmark song, if he ever composes lyrics from personal experience, he comments dryly, "Well, you know, I've never stood on a balcony in Argentina wearing a dress and singing to the proletariat. So, no, I do have to use my imagination"—referring, of course, to his watershed song from "Evita."

And what does Sir Tim Rice consider makes "I'll Never Smile Again" stand out?

"It's a good tune," he says. "It registers with people when they hear it: it sinks in. It's reassuring too. It's a mood people can identify with, which is very important. People may think, *I'm* in that situation, and it's consoling to know other people have been there too. But it's a wonderful lyric as well. You know, lyric writing can be tough. I find funny songs easier to write than love songs, because love songs have been written so many times, and you're left wondering what you can do to be new and different? To find a new way of saying it? But if you're writing something pretty corny, it's more of an open canvas. A word like 'icebox' or 'forklift truck' or 'giraffe,'—they won't fit easily into a love song. But these are words that actually add to the enjoyment of a funny song."

Alex Pangman

If you distil it, it has all the hallmarks of a very great song.

So many artists have recorded "I'll Never Smile Again," so let's find out from a singer's standpoint what makes it such a standout number.

Alex Pangman, who has suffered from cystic fibrosis and is quite literally living with her third set of lungs as a result of transplants, sings in a breathy style made popular by early jazz vocalists. She's a proud Canadian and always happy to recognize her country's soul mates. "A book about Ruth Lowe?" she says, enjoying a cup of tea in her downtown Toronto century house. "Amazing! Fantastic! This is a story people should hear."

Asked about her current health situation, she says, "I feel robust and possibly the best I've felt since I was 12."

But she wants to talk about music, not breathing.

"When I was growing up listening to the Backstreet Boys or Paula Abdul or whatever, I just found the music vapid, empty. And I found myself drawn to music that was more poetic, the older stuff."

As to her opinion on why "I'll Never Smile Again" resonated with the 1940s audience: "There is a cycle to things, you know. And I think, perhaps, the run of songs like 'We're In the Money' had had its day. Perhaps, the public was ready for a simple and direct lament. In context, historically, this is probably what gave it such weight. That, and you have a beautiful melody, and lyrics that are straight from the heart and very poetic. It's beautiful and simple. And you know, there's a familiarity about it that breeds happiness, even though it's a sad song."

Alex herself has recorded the tune for her album *New*. "I picked it to record because it's such a beautiful melody. I like the form of it. It's not the typical form. A lot of the songs I do are AABA pattern—main theme, repeat, middle section, back to main theme—but 'I'll Never Smile Again' is ABAC. So, I like doing songs that are not the usual form. People always love to hear, 'This was Frank Sinatra's big entree into the world.' It's a song that's pretty engrained in popular culture. It is simple, yet elegant. It's a very giving song. It just makes sense musically. There's a logic within it that is very pleasing to the ear."

Almost as an afterthought, this attractive, lively *chanteuse* adds, "You know, when I sing the song and think about never smiling again, I do know that Ruth *did* smile again, so that bounces around in my head too."

Sid Mark

> *It's a wonderful song. A great piece of music,*
> *Great heartfelt lyric.*

Say, should you happen to be in Philadelphia on a Sunday, do yourself a favor and tune in WPHT, 1210, from 9 am to 1 pm. There, you'll find a show that is America's longest running radio program with the same host: "Sunday With Sinatra" featuring the irrepressible Sid Mark.

Now, understand that with Mr. Mark, we're talking a guy who enjoyed a 30-year personal relationship with Frank Sinatra. Not only that, the man is the leading authority when it comes to Sinatra's music. He has the largest collection of Sinatra recordings anywhere outside of what was contained in Frank's own private vaults—in excess of 1,800 individual song titles on vinyl records and over 200 compact discs. "Millions of DJs play Sinatra, but not the way Sid Mark has," says radio personality Big Daddy Graham. "The key is his consistency and his loyalty."

Speaking of laudatory quotes, try this one on: "Sid is my kind of guy… He can separate fact from fiction, and he knows the music business inside and out." So said Mr. Sinatra himself. And virtually any recognized musician worth his or her notes will agree.

For all the glory and recognition, Sid Mark is somewhat self-effacing. Sitting in the radio studio, prepping his next show, and having been offered congratulations when WPHT re-ups his contract—which they've been doing for 60 years!—he says simply, "Well thanks, but it's all about ratings these days. You know, you don't bring in the audience, you don't get to stay on the air." Mind you, he does add, "I am indeed proud. It's been a long haul, but a good one."

Even after all that time, Sid Mark remains an unabashed fan of Frank Sinatra's singing. "It's the quality of the music," he says. "It's the songs. It's the way he sings them. No one else could do with a song what he did. And you know, back then, Frank was lucky to be picked up by Dorsey: it was the Cadillac of bands."

And where does this expert rank "I'll Never Smile Again"?

"You know, you can't rank it. It's like saying what's the best song ever? Or the best singer ever? But it's a wonderful song. A great piece of music. Great heartfelt lyric. Of course, people felt she'd written it for her husband killed in the war, but apart from that, it was such a great song. And it was Dorsey and Sinatra just hitting their stride. It truly is a great song in its own right. As is 'Put Your Dreams Away,' I might add."

And about just what makes a great song, Sid offers this: "It's the message. The content. What it's about that makes you think, sit up, and take notice. If a song can do that, it's a great song."

We shouldn't leave this conversation with Sid without hearing a bit about his relationship with the greatest singer of the 20th century.

"Back in 1966, Sinatra released an album with Count Basie performing at the Sands in Las Vegas," he recalls. "Well, I played it continuously on the air and Philadelphia-area stores couldn't keep it on the shelves. Remember, this was the time of the British Invasion being in full force with the Beatles in their prime. But fans still were going nuts for Sinatra. So, all of a sudden, I get a call from someone in Sinatra's camp, and they're looking to show gratitude for all the exposure I'm providing. 'Do you want a TV set?' they ask me. And I say, 'No, I already have a TV set,'"

Sid laughs at this memory, then explains he told the caller that what he'd really like is to meet Sinatra one day.

"So, I get a call back, and I'm being invited out to Vegas to meet the man. Now, I have to tell you, this was at the beginning of my career: I was making peanuts, and I couldn't begin to afford a trip like that. So, I turn them down. Meanwhile, the New York

Times has called Sinatra the highest paid performer in the history of show business. 'You don't understand,' the guy says, 'When you are a guest of Mr. Sinatra, you are *his* guest. Don't worry about it.'"

Sid Mark is flown out to Vegas where he spends a weekend and hangs out with Frank Sinatra. The axiom that it's usually not a good idea to meet your heroes because disappointment is inevitable need not apply here. "Meeting Sinatra changed my life," he says. "I had reached the summit." And that relationship continued for over 30 years.

At the time of this conversation, the 100th anniversary of Sinatra's birth looms.

"Honestly, I thought he'd still be here," Sid says wistfully. "He seemed to have that fortitude. His last show, in Palm Springs in 1995, it was one of his best. As he was coming offstage, he said 'I think I'm ready to go back on the road.'"

Just before we leave this segment on Sid Mark, it's worth stating that he's only missed one show in his entire broadcast history. That was in 1999: he went in for open heart surgery.

And some other quick quips about I'll Never Smile Again":

Frank Sinatra

If this song is a lament at the loss of love, I get an ache in my gut. I feel the loss myself and I cry out the loneliness, the hurt, and the pain that I feel.

Nancy Sinatra

That song followed my dad his whole life, and I think it was probably because so many people identified with it in the first place. There's a reason *why* "I'll Never Smile Again" became a classic that has endured: it was a perfect song, interpreted by the perfect singer, at the perfect time. It was a meeting of honesty—the fundamental quality that my dad possessed—and the heartfelt, plaintive cry of a young, grieving widow." (And to Tom

Sandler, when he and Nancy met: "Tommy, most people would give their eye teeth to have *one* hit with my dad... your mom had *two*!!").

Frank Sinatra Jr.

When we were on the road doing concerts, Sinatra would often talk with the musicians about what a wonderful song it was. He said its eeriness was heartbreaking. And he's right: beautiful tune, wonderful lyrics—a true standard.

Quincy Jones

I was in Toronto attending a performance when I met Ruth Lowe's son. I practically fell out of my chair! I told him that "I'll Never Smile Again" was literally one of the songs that inspired my career. I mean, his mother had written one of the most famous songs in the world!

Sean Jones, singer

It's like "Somewhere Over the Rainbow": it just pulls you in. I can *sink* into that song. "I'll Never Smile Again" is so passionate, and that's what connects me to it.

Miles Raine, saxophonist

It's right up there with the best songs of the Great American Song Book, no question.

David Clayton-Thomas

It's so well-written. It's a melody you can't get out of your head once you've heard it. It's totally honest. I can't imagine it being a better song. Neither could Frank Sinatra. He said many times it was his favourite song, the one he loved to sing the most in concert.

Mark Steyn, writer

It's so beautifully written and lushly confident you don't even notice the structure. But in a broader sense, Ruth's ballad of love and loss and loneliness, torn from her own widowhood, caught the mood of Americans in that pensive interlude between the start of World War Two and their own entry into it. It succeeds not just as a song of bereavement but also as a song that captures the fragility of all wartime romance.

Murray Ginsberg, musician, author

I know that "I'll Never Smile Again" was recorded by other bands, like Glenn Miller and several others, but I do believe the reason it became the popular song it ultimately did was because of Frank Sinatra, that marvellous arrangement, and the tempo. Certainly, that had something to do with it.

Kim Stockwood, singer

One of the most heartbreakingly beautiful songs ever written. Very romantic, very dreamy, very wonderful, but very sad.

Spencer Leigh, British author and commentator

A song like "I'll Never Smile Again" needs someone to really interpret it, and that was Sinatra. He was one of the greatest interpreters of the popular song that ever lived. It's an extremely good song. It's right up there near the top. A good song is one that can be done by lots of people, and this song was covered by all the British dance bands back in the day. And, yes, she did write both the words and the music, but when you think that most of the other songs hailed from Broadway, there were always teams putting on those shows, teams writing the songs. "I'll Never Smile Again" is one of the few songs of the early 1940s that was just written as a song, not to support a show. So, Ruth was unique at that time. And it's such a great title too: grabs your interest before you even hear it.

Andy Kim, singer-songwriter

Any songwriter would give their eyeteeth to have *one* song performed by Frank Sinatra. But to have two songs that Frank not only performed but continued to perform and made standards out of is a pretty amazing accomplishment. She's already achieved more than a plaque. She found a way into your heart. What she created was beyond manmade. The song is beyond those awards.

Will Friedwald, author (whose newest book *The Music of Nat King Cole: Straighten Up and Fly Right* debuts soon)

It's a really good song. An outstanding song. A great Canadian song. I mean, it would be too much an apples-and-oranges thing to compare it to, say, an Irving Berlin number or something like that, but it sure was the perfect song for Sinatra to sing in that period. If anything, the song's appeal might be limited because it can't really be done in a different way: it's a slow ballad and I can't imagine it as any kind of an up-tempo number.

But you know, one thing that occurs to me is that every year on Canada Day, in July, here in New York, there's a big concert and they have a whole program of songs by Canadian songwriters. And there's Joni Mitchell and Leonard Cohen and that group. But there's *nothing* from the Great American Songbook! Why is that? After the folk-rock period, there are a ton of Canadian composers and performers that they showcase. But where is Canadian theatrical composer Sheldon Brooks who wrote some of the biggest hits of the early part of the 20th century—notably "Some of These days," which was picked up by Sophie Tucker and used as her theme song for 55 years? Where is Ruth Lowe? Why are they not featured? Because, man! She really had it together with "I'll Never Smile Again," that's for sure!

Toronto Globe and Mail

"Ruth Lowe: One of the most celebrated songwriters of the 20th century."

Figure 24: Chuck Granata

Chapter Nine

Chuck Granata

*I don't see how you can improve on perfection.
And that song to me is truly perfection.*

You're hearing the words of Chuck Granata, talking about "I'll Never Smile Again." If you're a student of music, or just someone with an abiding interest in the Great American Songbook, you'll know that name. He's a musical treasure trove of information, trivia, facts, and details.

More than that, though, Chuck's got a wonderful ability to sum up the big band era with detailed certainty, something he does regularly on *Nancy For Frank*, the radio program he produces with Nancy Sinatra.

Let's listen in as Chuck talks with author Peter Jennings...

Peter Jennings: Chuck, before we discuss Ruth Lowe and Frank Sinatra's signature tunes that she wrote for him, I do want to congratulate you on your wonderful book, *Sessions With Sinatra*.

I felt like I was actually there in the studio when Frank made those landmark records. You did such a wonderful job recreating those moments.

Chuck Granata: Aw, thanks, Peter, I appreciate that. Yeah, that was my aim, to let you, the reader, be a fly on the wall, seeing how all this music went down.

PJ: Well, you certainly achieved that in spades. OK, let's turn to "I'll Never Smile Again" by Ruth Lowe. No one knows Sinatra's music like you do, so tell me about your thoughts on this song. Let's start with, where would you place it in the five thousand or more tunes comprising the Great American Songbook?

CG: Absolutely in the top tier. It is one of those songs that even today, you can't help but stop and marvel at it because it's so expressive. It really comes from the heart, and it speaks to *everyone*, the feelings of everyday men and women. There's no getting around the fact that anyone could be in that position of losing someone. It's simple, it's elegant, and it's timely: so, I would absolutely put "I'll Never Smile Again" in the top 100 standards of all time.

PJ: Wow, that's lavish praise indeed. I know Tommy Sandler will be thrilled to hear that. You know, Chuck, one thing I always wonder about is with most of the standards being composed by song writing teams, Ruth, of course, wrote this one on her own, words and music. Do you think she could have done better had she paired up with someone?

CG: No. There's no—how do I say this—there's no deficiency in that song at all. The melody is beautiful. The lyrics are perfect. I mean, she nailed it. I don't think it could have been any better if she collaborated with someone. It might have been different, but better? No way. I don't see how you can improve on perfection. And that song to me is truly perfection.

PJ: So, tell me what, in your opinion, makes a good song, a perfect song? Can you put it into words?

CG: It takes a good melody to start with. Depending on whether it's a ballad or an up-tempo tune, that melody has to make you feel something. It has to tug at your emotional heartstrings, make you want to dance or be happy or be sad. But that's just the *entrée*. The lyrics are most important. It's that combination of a lyric that speaks to you and makes you think: "Ah. I have felt that way." And then, you mix in the emotional tug of the melody that pulls that lyric along: I think the combination of those two things are what make a great song.

PJ: Well said.

CG: You know, Peter, when you think of great songs, I think of Johnny Mercer and "I Remember You." Or Cole Porter: "I've Got You Under My Skin" or "Night and Day." Or Dorothy Fields and Jerome Kern's "The Way You Look Tonight." And you add to that group Ruth Lowe with "I'll Never Smile Again." These are all world class melodies and lyrics that make you not just feel something, but they make you want to go back and listen again. Those songs are the ones you never get tired of listening to because they *mean* something. And they help demarcate a place and a time for many people and evoke such strong memories. And they also speak to the future. These are songs that are played at weddings today. And they will be for years to come.

PJ: So, not songs like "Pimp My Ride" that won the Oscar a few years ago?

CG: (laughing) Oh please! You know what? I really wonder if songs like that will be any kind of memory 50 years from now. I don't think so. But songs like Ruth's sure will be, because they have that rare combination of melody and lyrical sentiment that is lasting.

PJ: Chuck, you have such a wealth of knowledge about the big band era when "I'll Never Smile Again" was introduced. Share with me a bit about what was going on then and how this song broke through.

CG: Well, I think, at that moment, the world was on the precipice of war and certainly American servicemen were enlisting and some were even beginning to go overseas. They were missed by their families and their significant others. They were quite young. And that ballad and that lyric resonated with them. It was as much a product of the moment as it was of personal sentimentality. I also think that even though there were some wonderful ballads that were being performed by Frank Sinatra—I think specifically of Frank Loesser's "Say It," one of my favourites from that time— "I'll Never Smile Again" was more personal. Every listener could relate to what the lyrics were saying. And, certainly, Frank Sinatra was poised at that time to be the premier interpreter of those lyrics. So, what Tommy Dorsey and Sinatra and Jo Stafford and the Pied Pipers achieved with that record was this incredibly personal sentiment that just resonated with the public and certainly with people who were missing their loved ones.

PJ: Could someone else have sung that song as well as Sinatra at the time? Or was it his song?

CG: Anyone could have certainly sung it, but it was a matter of whether they could have brought that very personal dimension to it that Sinatra was able to do. He had that ability—the inner sentiment, the inner meaning of a lyric—better than anyone at that time. So, while others could have introduced it, I don't think anyone could have given it the justice it deserved better than Frank Sinatra. Even though he was still a relatively unknown quantity at the time, it was pivotal in bringing his voice and his persona to the forefront, but it also helped cement his image as a romantic crooner.

PJ: I know you've got some thoughts on the role Tommy Dorsey played in making the song a hit.

CG: Well, here you have Dorsey's band—a pretty hot, swinging band—and they are employing this vocalist. And, at that time, the vocalist was more of an accessory than the feature of the big bands. The focus of most of the big bands was the band leader's instrument. You listen to the Dorsey recordings—especially the ones from 1940 and '41—and you hear that right at the start: Dorsey takes a trombone solo. He's clearly the face of the band. But that started to change: the trombone was supplanted by Sinatra's vocal, so that *he* now became the face of the band.

Dorsey had a pretty good ego, but he realized he could bring notoriety to the band by bringing the singer up front, making the vocalist the feature of the orchestra. Which Dorsey did beautifully, and it's a testament to the fact that it was Frank Sinatra who suggested to Dorsey that he bring strings into the band. Not many of the big bands did that. It was such a perceptive suggestion because that really set the Dorsey band apart, and it also set Sinatra up as a vocalist with that string cushion. He was able to really emote a whole different level in terms of sensitivity and expressiveness. And no one knew better than Axel Stordhal (Dorsey's chief arranger) how to write for those strings. And Fred Stulce, a member of the band, was quite capable of arranging for strings too and did so beautifully.

PJ: I think another thing that made their recording of "I'll Never Smile Again" so special is that it featured the Pied Pipers behind Frank as part of the main arrangement of the song.

CG: Absolutely. So, now you have this confluence of elements: you have this soft, romantic, and expressive lyric line, beautifully arranged with the vocal chorus and Frank Sinatra right up front, and it just came along at the right moment. It really spoke to people who needed to hear that kind of almost plaintive, lonely lyric that meant something to them. And that really was the beginning of people sitting up and taking notice of Frank Sinatra as a vocalist, as a crooner, and it also helped to create a whole new sound for the Dorsey band.

PJ: Timing played a role, right?

CG: It was all a matter of timing: you have a wonderful song—an important song—in the hands of a very capable vocalist with one of the number one bands in the country—if not *the* number one band—and then the added bonus of having the push from Billboard listing the song as #1. It all helped move Frank Sinatra into that limelight where he was, all of a sudden, in the spotlight as the man. And, I think, honestly if you really think about it, that was the beginning of the end of the big bands.

PJ: Really. How so?

CG: Let's face it: when the big bands were really hot in the late 30s and early 40s, the focus was on the melody played by the band leader, whoever that happened to be—Glenn Miller, or Artie Shaw, or Tommy Dorsey. People weren't really focusing on the lyrics because these were dance aggregations. People would go to the Hotel Pennsylvania in New York City or the Glen Island Casino on Long Island or the Palladium Ballroom in Los Angeles, and they would go to dance. They weren't necessarily keying in on a vocalist. But what happened is that when Sinatra took to the microphone on those dance dates, everybody stopped and began to watch him, and that, I believe, is why Frank was such a great showman because he did so many of those dance dates and the one-nighters with the Dorsey band. He learned how to sing to an audience. So, we see this shift from big bands serving to be dance bands—being the background for people dancing—to almost becoming mini concerts where people would come now to see the vocalist—to see and hear Frank Sinatra. And I say "see him" because people would actually stop dancing and watch him.

PJ: I get it. Because of this, the bands were being replaced by the vocalist.

CG: Right. And what happened is, Dorsey was brilliant. Not only was he a great instrumentalist—not only did he bring together the very best musicians in the world for that band—but he also taught Sinatra how to be a showman.

You know, Peter, if you think back, before Dorsey, the bands would have their singer just sitting there ready to croon when called upon. There was no surprise, it was all right in front of you and what was expected. But what Dorsey did is he kept the featured vocalist behind the scenes. So, the band would begin to play and when it was Sinatra's time to sing, he would actually come out from the wings, as though something special was happening. It's far more dramatic, with a song like "I'll Never Smile Again," to start the tune and then bring out your vocalist. It makes it more of a show, and that's what Dorsey really did at that moment. He changed the way people presented their bands. Dorsey really started to *present* the featured vocalist, and even a featured instrumentalist, by making it an event. And those little elements of showmanship were what Frank Sinatra learned early on.

So, that brought about the focus on the singer and the beginning of the end of the big bands. The singer was now the centre of attention, not the band.

I've always wondered if Dorsey would do the same thing if he knew what the outcome was going to be.

PJ: Chuck, what about Ruth's other song for Sinatra: his theme song?

CG: "Put Your Dreams Away": it's equally beautiful. I don't think the sentiment could be better put. It was a wonderful closing theme for Sinatra, and he clearly recognized that from very early on, from almost the beginning of his solo career and his radio career because he used it as his closing theme and continued to do that up until the mid 1960s when he had those great "A Man and His Music" TV specials, and he closed those with "Put Your Dreams Away." And, of course, it was played at his funeral, the last tune as people left the church. I should add that Nancy chose that song to end her weekly show on SIRIUS Radio each time. It again is such a beautiful sentiment with such a wonderful meaning. I put it in the same class as "I'll Never Smile Again." They're very different, the catalysts for one being a very sad situation and the other one really does speak of hope and optimism, but I love the song and I know it's one of Nancy's favourite songs.

PJ: Parting thoughts?

CG: You know, I'm kind of surprised that Ruth didn't write more songs for Sinatra and other singers.

PJ: Truth be told, I think she got tired of all the hoopla in New York and L.A. and yearned for the simpler life back in Toronto. There, she married a stockbroker who was not at all keen on the showbiz kind of stuff, so she really gave it up and became a society chatelaine. She had two kids and enjoyed a wonderful, very full life. But when you consider those two songs, I agree. I'm sure there were others in her, but it just wasn't the way the cards were laid out.

CG: Interesting, I didn't know that. But let me share one other thought with you. I always thought "I'll Never Smile Again" has a very Mercer-like quality. Those are lyrics that, if I didn't know who they were written by, I'd guess Johnny Mercer. It's that kind of quality. Mercer spoke to everyone too. Mercer wrote for the common man: you didn't have to be sophisticated and highbrow to get the lyric line as you did sometimes with, for instance, Cole

Porter. Mercer's lyrics were plain and simple, and the expression is always right up front.

That, and when you consider Sinatra recorded "I'll Never Smile Again" four times: well, you gotta know he felt the song had legs. There was the original with the Dorsey band, then the movie version, then with Gordon Jenkins in 1959 for that devastating album *No One Cares,* and then, again, for Reprise in 1965 for *A Man and His Music*. I mean, the fact that he recorded it all those times, each time with a different reading, that, in itself, has to say something about its importance.

Thanks, Chuck Granata. It's always a pleasure to partake in such knowledge and informed opinion.

PART TWO

Chapter Ten

A New Love. A New Life.

It's been written there are no second acts in American lives.

But for a young, attractive Canadian gal, full of *chutzpah*, there was no need to consider such limitations. Indeed, a brilliant Act Two was about to unfold for Ruth Lowe back home in Toronto.

Life on Broadway—"The Great White Way"—had taken Ruthie and Mickey on a roller coaster ride neither of them could ever have imagined. The craziness of interviews, radio appearances, autograph signings, meetings with music publishers, and regular *kibitzing* with other songwriters frequenting Tin Pan Alley was–well–crazy!

Still, after a while, it began to pale.

"Mom told me she'd got to the point where fun was fun, but this had become a little much," Tommy Sandler recalls. "At heart, she was still a young, somewhat innocent Toronto girl who'd had her heart broken when her husband died. She'd been robbed of the simple life she yearned for. Not that she took the New York lifestyle for granted or would have passed it by. But it was relentless, and maybe a little overwhelming for her. It had lost its allure. It didn't really offer her the secure life she knew she ultimately needed. And, you know, I think she was at the point where she wanted to meet someone and settle down, and that wasn't likely to happen in New York."

And so, Ruth and Mickey packed their bags and headed home.

It didn't take long for love to show its face again.

He was 36. He lived at home with his parents. He was the oldest of five boys.

In fact, when they met, Nat Sandler had already been fixed up some time before on a blind date with Ruth Lowe, this ingénue who was still living in New York City but was back for the holidays. He'd got cold feet at the last minute and stood her up.

Now, here he is at a function at a Lake Simcoe resort, and there she is.

Cookie Sandler, Ruth's daughter-in-law (married to Tom's older brother Stephen), takes it from there...

Figure 25: Sandler-Lowe marriage announcements

"So, here they are, at a party and she arrives with a lawyer she'd met. Well, Nat's not too happy about this. Nor is he pleased with himself, for having stood her up previously, now that he gets a look at this pretty lady. Turns out he knows the lawyer slightly: so, he goes up to him and tells him to get lost. Amazingly, the guy takes off, leaving the way open for Nat. He then pleads his case to Ruth and invites her to his house to see his dog. Ruth's no pushover and figures it's one of those, 'Wanna come up and see

my etchings' kind of thing. But she decides to go anyway and is
amazed when they arrive and he says, 'Here's my dog'".

"So, there she is, patting the animal when, all of a sudden,
Nat's parents walk in.

"She realizes he lives there. With them.

"And the penny drops: this isn't an ulterior motive kind of
liaison.

"No sir. And just two months later, Ruth and Nat get married."

With this new, loving union in place, the question was: would
Ruth continue with her music career? Would she welcome
childbirth? Would the role of chatelaine be appropriate?

Having shed the enormous influence of Broadway, just what
was her new role to be back home in Toronto?

One thing certain: with Nat now starting to do well from his
brokerage business, and with royalties regularly appearing in the
mail based on Ruth's published songs, life presented wonderful
options to the affable couple.

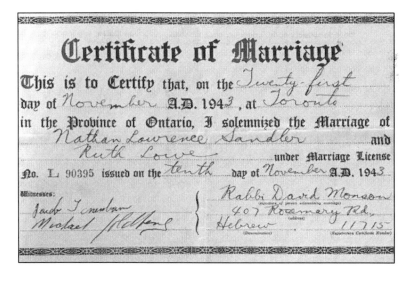

Figure 26: Sandler-Lowe Marriage Certificate

"I do know she missed the limelight," says Aline Sandler, Tom's wife. "I mean, it's hard for a performer not to perform. Don't get me wrong: she loved her life, she loved Nat, and she loved her children and grandchildren. But you can't replace the celebrity experience she'd been through, you just can't. There's always that little part of you that says, 'What if I had stayed and gone to California?' or 'What if I'd performed more?' or..."

"Mom wanted to have a family life, she really did," says Tom Sandler. "But I think she also wanted to have another hit song. It played on her from time to time. You could tell."

"She really loved her grandchildren," adds Aline. "She was so close with them. She was so happy to see them, to be with them. And Nat too: he loved the grandchildren. They were both very hands-on with the grandkids."

"You know, my mother and step-father met Ruthie and Nat before I did," explains Aline. "In fact, they met Tommy before I did. The two couples were at a wedding, began chatting, and hit it off. Then, Ruth and Nat go to Florida, and my mom and stepfather go too, and darned if they don't meet there again.

"There are so many flukes," says Aline. "I mean, here I am separating from my husband and moving from Montreal to Toronto. I don't know anyone in Toronto. So, I end up renting an apartment at a place called Leaside Towers in the suburb of Don Mills. My mom had given me Ruthie's name, so I call her and say, 'My name is Aline Plotnick and my mom said to call you and say hi.' And Ruth, being Ruth, immediately invites me for lunch. She says, 'Where do you live?' '85 Thorncliffe Park Drive,' I reply. To which she says—and get this—she says, 'Well, I live at 95 Thorncliffe Park Drive! Right next door. We're neighbors!' I mean, talk about coincidence. It's a big city. I could have moved anywhere. But obviously this was meant to happen.

"So, I went to lunch and before long she's showing me photos, including of Tommy. I discovered that he lived downstairs from them. And I saw he had long hair and played the guitar! Well, I was smitten! He was only 23 years old and I was older, but that didn't matter.

"This was March 15th, 1973. Over 45 years ago—hard to believe."

"I spent a lot of time with Ruth," Cookie Sandler says. She considers she's one lucky lady. "You know, lots of people have to put up with their in-laws. But I drew the ace card with Ruthie and Nat. I just loved them both! I didn't come from the same lifestyle that she had adopted, but she taught me so much. I met Steve when I was 14, started hanging out at their cottage at Lake Simcoe by 15, 16. I loved everything she did. I had a very close relationship with her. We traveled together. I learned that she was not a great housekeeper. *Everybody* seemed to know her. She was a very generous woman. And she had what she used to call '*F. You* money.' If her husband told her she couldn't have something, she'd say, '*F. You*' and go out and buy it for herself with her own money. From the time I was 16, because she didn't have a daughter, I kind of took over that spot. If she was buying eye shadow, she'd buy two and give me one. She was always doing things like that, because her friends had daughters and she didn't. So, she treated me like her daughter. I loved her. I had fun with her. The times we had at the cottage are special memories."

Mind you, there were walls of privacy that even this closeness was not about to penetrate.

"I remember asking her once, 'So Ruthie, between the time when your husband died in 1939 and the time when you married Nat in 1943, did you have any lovers?' And she turned red and spat out, "None of your business!' And that was the end of that!"

"Looking back, Ruthie was always very stylish," says Aline. "She had been since she was younger, and she kept that up. She had lovely clothes and shoes and bags and things. She cared about how she looked, and she always looked very stylish. She shopped at Creeds: she knew the Creed family, so she liked to shop there."

Indeed, Edmond Creed had an infallible eye for fashion and loved showcasing it in the family's elegant store on Toronto's home of chic: Bloor Street.

"Eddie was a real fashion guy," his son says. "He was interested in creating design—I don't know where he got his drawing ability. Even though the store closed in 1990, women of style still mourn that day."

"I can tell you that Ruthie never sat still for long," says Aline. "She was always busy with something. She was definitely not the type of person to stay home a lot. She wanted to keep busy. She loved to go out in the evening, and so we went out a lot with her and Nat. She loved playing cards: those stories are many!

"She was very spontaneous. We'd be at La Scala for dinner and without even a word, she'd get up and start playing the piano. She'd play when we came for dinner. I loved it."

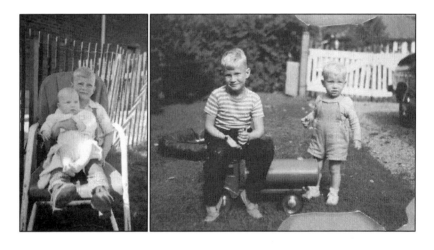

Figure 27: Stephen and Tommy

Where Ruth was more flamboyant and fun-loving, Nat was conservative.

"Very simply, he was a stockbroker, and he loved that life," explains Aline. "He was very serious. He had mellowed with age once he retired, but he was still a serious man. He did love to go out in the evenings, and he could be a lot of fun. And he was very good to all of us. You could have fun with him."

Ruth expressed love differently to both Steve and Tom because they were both totally different personalities. Tom was closer to his mom because of his creativity, and Steve was closer to his father because of being in business.

But one fact was clear: Ruthie loved them both equally, and very much.

Chapter Eleven

Toronto Vitality. Lake Simcoe Verve.

It's the poker games that have become the stuff of legends.

You see, as Ruth settled into becoming a homemaker in a well-to-do area of Toronto, her sense of fun, adventure, and gaiety led to getting together with "the girls" to play cards. No doubt this was a holdover from those interminable days on the band bus with Ina Ray Hutton's Melodears where smoking and card playing were the pastimes that kept the girls from killing their wanderlust.

Figure 28: Valentine's Day Card

"But I can go one better," says Bonnie Levy. "My mom, Luba Bronstein, often acted as hostess for these games. And I will never forget coming home from school—I was, maybe, 13 or 14—

and through the clouds of smoke what do I see but eight noisy, crazy ladies sitting at the table in our dining room trying to scalp each other at poker, all the while *dressed in their bras*!! No tops, just their bras!"

Seems dealing with the sweats of menopause had become the pre-poker discussion point until one of the ladies—"most likely Ruthie," says Bonnie, "I mean, I'm sure it would have been Ruthie"—suggested they remove their tops to play in comfort. "It was a popular resolve, my mom told me. This amongst the screams of laughter, incessant smoking, and the odd pull from a scotch bottle."

Bonnie then confesses that she thought *everyone* played cards this way, yelling at each other, playing in their brassieres, smoking to beat the band, and enjoying their drams of hooch.

"It's funny, you just accepted it," she says about Ruth's fame. "She wasn't one to make a big noise about it. But you just knew that was part of her. That she'd written a song Frank Sinatra had sung. I just thought about her as someone who was perky, quirky, blonde, lots of fun. She was someone who always made you feel comfortable. She always wanted to know about *you*.

"I'll tell you this: it was special when Ruthie played the piano," Bonnie continues. "She brought everybody together in a merry style. She could play anything at all. There'd be singsongs involved. It was always started with her being encouraged to play for us, and then, off we'd go. It just made you happy. *She* made me happy. She seemed to make it her life's aim to make everybody happy. She was awesome!"

And then, we have this from Wendy Eisen: "Ruth and my mother, Allie Herman, were really good friends. I knew her through that relationship. She was part of our lives. To know someone famous who had written a hit parade song was very special back then. Ruth had a great sense of humour. Always smiling, always laughing. A lot of fun. Of all my mother's friends, she was the least serious.

"I do remember one particular time when the ladies had played cards very late into the wee small hours. It's 2 am when Ruth gets home. Now, Nat rolls over in bed and she's afraid he's going to wake up and ask her what time it is. So, she jumps into bed with her clothes on—high heels and everything!"

From that point on, if it was an evening game, the girls would don their nightgowns and dressing gowns, go over to someone's house, play cards, and then come home and go to sleep: Ruth would have started that for sure.

"My mother told me this story," says Wendy. "Seems there was a dinner in New York where they invited composers and professors. A somewhat strange combination. Anyway, Ruth was at the head table because 'I'll Never Smile Again' was on the hit parade and here was this sweet, adorable girl who'd written it. So, she's sitting there, and the man beside her asks about her song. As only Ruth could, she goes into explaining how when most people write songs, they write the melody and then they write the bridge: but she wrote the bridge first. And then, she goes into detail explaining the mechanics of song writing and all that stuff. Finally, she turns to him and says, 'And what university are you associated with?' He responds, 'I'm not. My name is Oscar Hammerstein.' And he gets up and walks off."

"So, there we have young Ruth Lowe from Toronto taking one of Broadway's most prolific songwriters to school on how to write songs!"

In some ways, Tom Sandler's home today doubles as a museum for his mom. Her old piano still sits in the living room, the sunny-yellow paint supporting a cluster of family photos. And Ruth Lowe's honorary Grammy, presented a year after her death in 1981, hangs on the wall beside a glamorous portrait of the famed songwriter.

Figure 29: Tom with Percy Faith's recording

Asked about his first memory of his mom, Tommy recounts how at age 5, he appeared with her on "This Is Your Life," First created as a radio show in 1948, then moving to the new medium of television in 1952 where it remained on the air until 1961, the program featured the show's creator and host, Ralph Edwards, who would surprise some unsuspecting person—often celebrities like Marilyn Monroe, Bob Hope, Jayne Mansfield, Andy Griffith, et al. He would review the subject's personal and professional life in front of the TV audience, introducing figures from their past as live guests. The show drew great interest from viewers, partly because the identity of the subject wasn't revealed until the show went live.

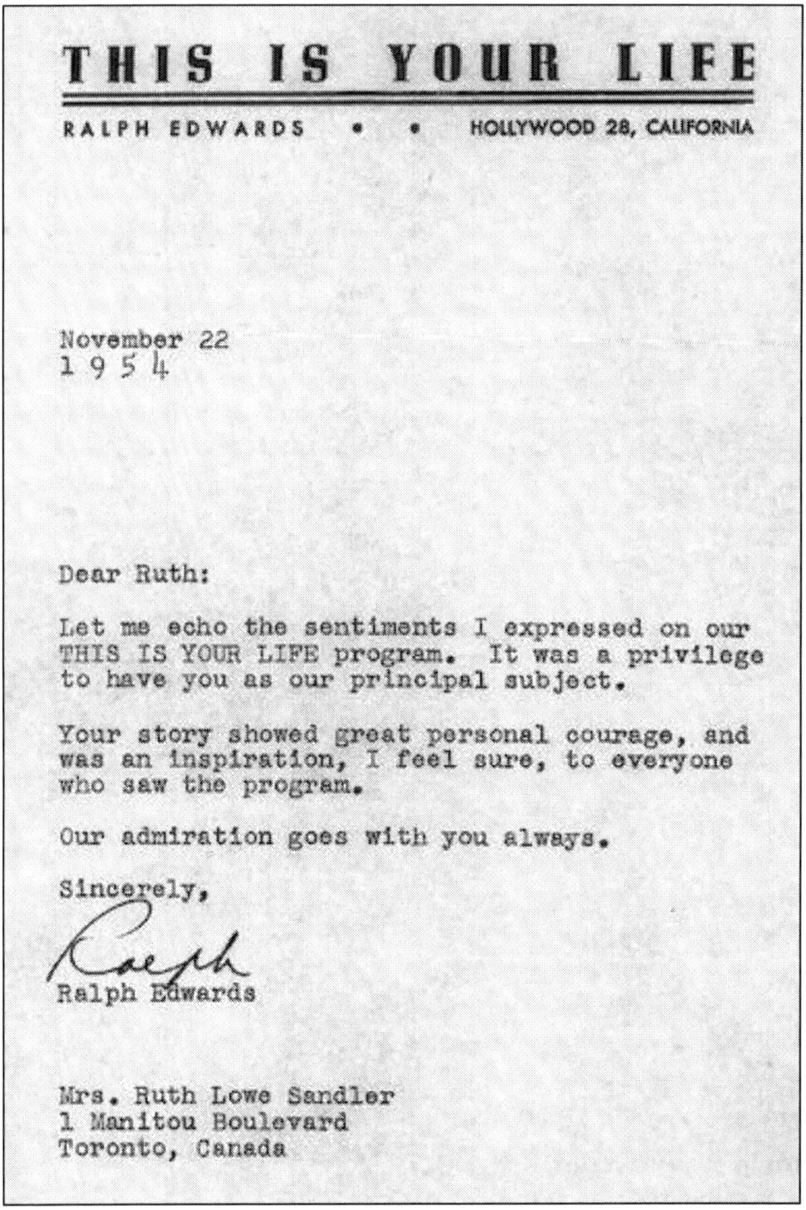

THIS IS YOUR LIFE

RALPH EDWARDS • • HOLLYWOOD 28, CALIFORNIA

November 22
1 9 5 4

Dear Ruth:

Let me echo the sentiments I expressed on our
THIS IS YOUR LIFE program. It was a privilege
to have you as our principal subject.

Your story showed great personal courage, and
was an inspiration, I feel sure, to everyone
who saw the program.

Our admiration goes with you always.

Sincerely,

Ralph Edwards

Mrs. Ruth Lowe Sandler
1 Manitou Boulevard
Toronto, Canada

Figure 30: This Is Your Life letter from Ralph Edwards

Figure 31: This Is Your Life

"It was a big secret to my mom," recalls Tommy. "They told her she was going to Hollywood to do an interview with Variety Magazine. That was the ruse they used to get her there. And then they flew me and my brother and my Aunt Mickey out there separately. They wanted us on the show, but we weren't allowed to tell my mom *anything*—not an easy secret for a five-year-old to keep! They kept us hidden in the hotel room because they didn't want Mom to see that we were there. And you know, it was a real eye-opener for me—made me realize my mom was a big deal.

"Of course, as only mom could, when she's surprised by Ralph Edwards and told she's starring live on 'This Is Your Life,' she clutches at her hair and says, 'I wish I knew. I'd have had a bleach!'

"Best line of all time!" laughs Bonnie Levy.

"I grew up being really happy in Toronto," says Tommy. "It was nice to share the life I had. My mom was always really generous, and we lived in a very open, creative kind of atmosphere. I was encouraged to be creative and happy. And music was an amazing way to be able to connect with everything and open yourself up and be a full, complete person. So, I was brought up like that, and I always liked to share that with my friends. We lived in one of Toronto's affluent areas and most of my friends came from well-to-do families. But I just had this extra dimension in my life that was based on entertainment—show biz—it just added another level of good stuff to an already great life."

Usually in the evenings, after dinner, Ruth would sit at the piano and begin playing.

Tommy: "I used to love hearing her play. As a kid, I'd dance around the living room. It was wonderful. I'd spin around until I'd drop on the floor and mom would keep playing. She was always asking me what I wanted to hear. She was like a human juke box! I felt very close to her. We were like kindred spirits through the music and I don't think she had that same sense with my brother or my dad. They were more serious, more business-like. She saw the creative side in me and all she wanted to do was develop it and make me happy. I mean, music…it's a very healing force, a very friendly force. It was powerful...like a tonic almost. And she was a really excellent piano player. She could read, write, score— almost like a genius. When you have that kind of ability—when it's second nature—it's a great gift."

"Yes, it was a real legacy," says Steve Sandler. "In many ways, she was a crazy lady, always doing silly things, but always really interesting. Do you know the story about the sun tanning booth? She built...she got a platform on wheels and put up boards with reflective surfaces. And she'd lie in there to get a tan and she'd fall asleep. And she'd tie it up because our driveway was slanted. But, one day, it got loose and off goes mom, careening down the street in this crazy thing...

"All of my friends knew about her," Steve continues. "I would have told them. I still tell people. If I hear that tune played, I'll say, 'My mom wrote that song.' It feels pretty good to be able to do that."

Figure 32: Ruth's piano

At the end of the day, it was hard to keep a great talent down. Despite not working flat out on writing new songs, Ruth could get inspired by an event and, sure enough, a tune would soon be flowing from her creative imagination.

And so, it was that Lyndon Johnson, President of the U.S., gave a speech in the 1960s that talked about things he'd like to see happen that could lead to ending the war in Viet Nam. A recurring theme of Johnson's was, "And so do I, and so do I." This resonated with Ruth. "There's a song there," she said to herself and out flowed a tune with these lyrics that captured her hope for change:

> *The whole world wants to see a peaceful sky,*
> *And so do I, and so do I*
>
> *Everyone wants a rainbow way up high,*
> *And so do I, and so do I*
>
> *There is so much to give for*
> *Things that we hold so true.*
>
> *There is so much to live for*
> *For someone like you*
>
> *Everyone wants someone all their own*
> *To laugh and cry as years go by*
> *And so do I, and so do I.*[18]

Mind you, this was not the first nod to a President. Back in the 1940s, when Ruth was still in New York riding the coattails of fame, she had decided one day that it was her duty to write a song that would honor the First Lady, Franklin Roosevelt's wife, Eleanor. "Eleanor, First Lady of My Heart" was the result.

---

[18] Unpublished lyrics.

Now, Ruth Lowe was nothing if not a promoter of the first rank: it had been born into her soul by her father. She figured that if the President himself would endorse her song, she'd have it made as an instant hit. She also reasoned that since she was such a success with Sinatra and Dorsey, why not "double down" with the President and First Lady! But what she learned was that the President of the United States is never permitted to endorse or promote commercial ventures of any kind. Still, she wanted to honor Mrs. Roosevelt (and, hey, if by chance the President happened to put his presidential seal on the manuscript, well, that would be OK too). So, Ruth sends off "Eleanor, First Lady of My Heart" to the White House and settles in to wait. And wait. And wait. Finally, she gets word that the President and the First Lady are honored she has written the song. And that's it? Yup. It ends there, no presidential endorsement.

From the what-goes-around-comes-around department, Ruth figured this little nugget might yet live to see a more receptive day. So, she stuffed the tune into her piano bench and there it stayed for years. That is, until John Kennedy was elected President and together with his First Lady Jacqueline, they were capturing the inspiration of the public.

Always resourceful, Ruth realizes the name "Jacqueline" has the same number of syllables as "Eleanor": they're interchangeable! So, she pulls out the original manuscript, rewrites the song as "Jacqueline, First Lady of My Heart" and once again, she sends it to the White House. And, once again, she receives written acknowledgement that the President and First Lady appreciate the song, they are both fans of her music, "but, unfortunately, the President is not able to endorse a commercial venture."

Ruthie took the turn-down in stride (after all, been there, done that) and was gratified to at least receive a letter from the White House. "I'm also honored they are such big fans of my music," she confessed to her sister.

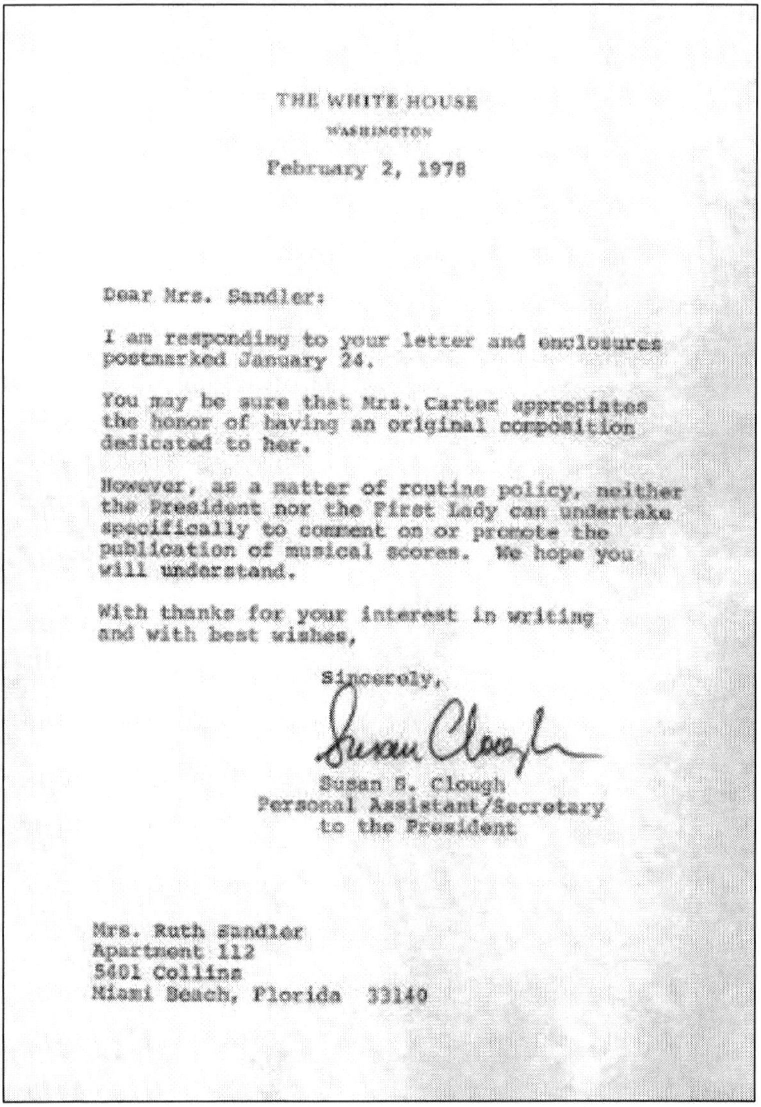

THE WHITE HOUSE

WASHINGTON

February 2, 1978

Dear Mrs. Sandler:

I am responding to your letter and enclosures postmarked January 24.

You may be sure that Mrs. Carter appreciates the honor of having an original composition dedicated to her.

However, as a matter of routine policy, neither the President nor the First Lady can undertake specifically to comment on or promote the publication of musical scores. We hope you will understand.

With thanks for your interest in writing and with best wishes,

Sincerely,

Susan S. Clough
Personal Assistant/Secretary
to the President

Mrs. Ruth Sandler
Apartment 112
5401 Collins
Miami Beach, Florida 33140

Figure 33: Letter from White House

Was there one more shot at this? You bet.

The 1970s roll around and Jimmy Carter now occupies the White House with his First Lady Rosalynn. Wouldn't you know it:

same number of syllables. "Rosalyn, First Lady of My Heart" is a slam dunk! So, Ruth re-writes the song to its new star and off it goes to Pennsylvania Avenue. And soon, she's reading a letter thanking her for honoring the first lady, saying they too are big fans of her music, but unfortunately the President cannot endorse her song.

Tom Sandler: "Mom was tenacious. Of course, she would have loved to have received a presidential endorsement, but that wasn't the only reason for writing the song. What was equally important was the thrill she got from composing a piece of music that honored the First Lady of the United States."

"Mom always inspired me to aim higher, reach further, and never be afraid. She once said, 'Tommy, reach for the stars. You'll probably touch some. But if you miss, you might just capture the moon!'"

"Now, if that's not a great title for a song..."

Meanwhile, Steve Sandler had ended up at N.L. Sandler and Company, working with his dad. Perhaps, that's why he's businesslike, not unlike his late father.

"What you learn from your father is to be honest with people, never screw anybody," says Steve. "The most important thing is your integrity. You never go back on your word: you never try to cheat anybody. He was well respected. You know, he was the first Jewish member of the Toronto Stock Exchange. But it was hard for me working together with him: it's never easy having a father and son working together. Different styles. You get into arguments. Still, I did learn the basics of the business because it was a very small firm and I got to try it all.

"You wouldn't consider him humorous," adds Steve, talking about his dad. "He was more stable. Maybe it was a case of opposites attract with him and Mom. But in terms of her success, I don't think he ever went crazy over it. He liked the income because she was more or less self-sufficient. But I never heard him bragging about her being a songwriter or anything."

Nat was determined to build his business. He worked a lot. And because he was already 45 years old when Tom was born, the young boy found it hard to connect with his father.

"He was a serious, heavy-duty business guy," says Tommy. "He was a protector. He was a big guy with a quick temper. He was always trying to run the house and have discipline and mom was always trying to protect us from that. He could be a little over-bearing. He wasn't a hands-on-parent kind of guy. But he provided an amazing house and cottage. He seemed pretty serious all the time. He was strict: old-school style. He kept a lot of things inside himself.

"And then, you have my mom. Very forward-thinking, very futuristic. We had a very modern house, ahead of its time. The whole place was wired with speakers. She had a guy build her this incredible, powerful hi-fi system. She had a huge speaker right in the foyer. She loved cool stuff—advanced, futuristic artwork. It was really trippy in our house because she had all these toys, hi tech gadgets, great artwork. Dad was preoccupied with work, so he didn't really appreciate it all. But he was definitely grateful for what she brought to our lives. She was always celebrating something!"

Meanwhile, the family began to embrace the cottage lifestyle with zest.

"I don't want you to think this is a shrine or anything," says Cookie Sandler as she shows off her Lake Simcoe home. "But my mother-in-law, Ruth, had such great taste, and I've incorporated a lot of what she had into this house.

"Ruth and I seemed to click. I know she and Aline clicked too. Ruthie was just that kind of person: very welcoming, very warm, very appreciative.

"For sure," says Aline. "She was always inviting us for dinner. She took us everywhere. We'd go to dinner at their place, or go out to dinner, or go to Florida, where we'd be with her and Nat and meet celebrities. She seemed to like to do that a lot. We had a very good relationship."

Cookie will never forget the time Ruth took her to New York.

"Here's a story for you. We're staying at the Waldorf Astoria, and Ruth and I have just come back from seeing a show and, all of a sudden, she says, 'Look, there's Frank!' And, sure enough, Frank Sinatra and his wife, Barbara, are about to go up to the private residences in the Waldorf. 'C'mon' says Ruth and she yanks me along with her. 'Frankie,' she yells across the hall. And he looks around and says, 'Ruthie!' He comes over, introduces us to Barbara, and they start chatting: you know, 'What are you doing here?', What's happening?' and, then, all of a sudden, Barbara says, 'Frank, we are expected upstairs.' And he looks cowed. And then, he says, 'Well Ruth, it was great seeing you.' And they leave. And Ruthie was not happy. 'What's wrong?' I asked. And she was so disappointed that he didn't invite her up. She really was hurt. But Barbara was not about to have that happen. They'd actually met up a few years earlier in Toronto when he was performing there, and she was invited backstage and the two of them had a wonderful time joking and showing off pictures of their grandchildren. And Frank was saying, 'We'll have to make a match with these kids," and she had such a great time with him.

"She wasn't staid at all: she liked to have fun. She was happy. Her life became her family and friends. She was sure known as a character."

"Absolutely!" says Lynda Rapp, thinking back. "Ruthie was so much fun. She was a very fun, fun-loving, perky lady. And very cute. But she had her serious side too: she was very charity minded. Of course, she was older than me, but that didn't stop her from doing anything. I remember at the Hadassah Bazaar, she sidles over to our booth wearing a black turtleneck that features the words printed out in sparkles, 'One Million Dollar Babe.' Omigosh! That was the kind of person she was: a party girl, fun loving.

"You know, she could have a potty mouth occasionally. And that was funny.

"But what I saw all the time was the great love she had for her children and for her daughters-in-law, both of whom she spoiled."

Chapter Twelve

Growing up Vaudeville

*You can take the girl out of show biz, but you
can't take show biz out of the girl.*

Tom Sandler

Tommy Sandler shares some memories...

Thinking about my mom has always made me smile and get encouraged. Consider that for a moment: how many people do you actually know whose memory brings a smile to your face? Well, that's my mom. She was one of a kind, the most positive and optimistic person you could ever meet, always encouraging me to be better, follow my dreams, to laugh, and, to experience the joys of living.

Mom would always bring back gifts for us when she was away, and I'm not talking boring handouts. I mean, if she went to New York, she'd come home with amazing toys and big bags of U.S. candy bars: Chunkies, Babe Ruth, American Snickers. She'd always go to FAO Schwarz and buy the coolest gifts. She loved to surprise everyone. Mom was very generous and good-hearted.

I also remember wonderful adventures with her. For instance, when my brother and I were just kids in the 1950s, we were in Miami and mom got us tickets to be on the Howdy Doody show. Now, you millennials may not recognize that name, but I have to tell you, back in the day, Howdy Doody was huge! This was *the* kids' TV series that started on NBC in 1947 and really began it all as a pioneer in children's television programming, setting the pattern for many future programs. Howdy Doody himself was a freckle-faced boy marionette, who hung out with a live character named Buffalo Bob Smith. And if you were lucky enough to be a kid in the small audience for the live TV show, you'd sit in the Peanut Gallery. So, there's me and Steve sitting quietly, right there in the Peanut Gallery and, all of a sudden, Buffalo Bob wanders over to ask us our names. On TV! I couldn't believe it. But not being one to miss an opportunity, I spoke out good and loud: "I'm Tommy. He's Steve." All on live TV. I remember mom being in the studio audience and almost fainting that I spoke!

I was really disappointed at the end of the show, thinking we'd get a gift or at least a box of candy. All we got was a mini box of Nabisco Shredded Wheat. Are you kidding me!? They were the sponsor! I never watched Howdy Doody again!

Life was exciting all the time with mom. She took me to Massey Hall, Toronto's famous venue for music, to attend a Duke Ellington concert featuring Ella Fitzgerald. I was 10, maybe 12. But the special part was going backstage to meet The Duke: man, he seemed 10 feet tall and the nicest guy ever. Mom loved going to Broadway plays so much and I saw many of them with her. She loved show biz so much.

Mom would tell me stories about the old days in vaudeville, like when she worked with comedian Red Skelton. Red did a skit called Guzzlers Gin where he fakes getting drunk by downing a whole bottle of gin at one time. Of course, there was water in the bottle. That is until one day, Mom and her friend replaced the water with real gin! Red comes on stage, grabs the bottle, and starts downing it. I remember her telling me that he got a few gulps in when it hit: Skelton turned fire engine red! Crazy stunt. She'd also tell me about following a comedian named Bert Wheeler on the stage. He did the old leaning act (first having bolted his shoes to the stage before the audience arrived.) and he'd lean out into the audience and get laughs. So, Mom, in her first performance, walks out on the stage, doesn't see the shoe bolts, trips over them, and does a swan dive right into the front row. What a way to make an entrance! But she'd tell me that story again and again, always laughing. She never took herself too seriously.

I also remember her telling me stories of how, on live radio, she'd crawl under the piano and tie the pianist's show laces together during the show. You can imagine what happened when he got up to leave. And then, there was the time she was part of a live theatrical performance with the Tommy Dorsey Orchestra. Dorsey and the band were on two separate hydraulic stages that came up from the floor. They were supposed to stop at stage level, of course. But something went wrong with the platform Dorsey was on: it kept going up. And up and up. And then, it got stuck up there and wouldn't come down. So, Tommy conducted the whole show from the rafters!

Another story about Tommy Dorsey (after whom I'm named): he had a live radio show in the early 1940s that Mom was a guest on. The show was called *Fame and Fortune*, and she was asked about writing "I'll Never Smile Again." By this time, it had already sold 400,000 copies of sheet music and half a million records. I remember Dorsey would end the show with the line, "Remember to become famous, but don't forget to get the money."

Here's another one that always made me laugh when Mom told it. She once worked with a conductor who had false teeth. During a show, his teeth fell out! Mom killed herself laughing telling that story, and she made me laugh too. Such a sweet soul she was.

Then, there was the time at home on Manitou Blvd: the doorbell rings, I rush to open the front door and there's Mom, eyes closed, leaning on the door frame with a fake arrow through her head. I went into shock, thinking it was the real thing. Fortunately, she opened her eyes and put her arms around me. She loved living and making people happy so much. In fact, her philosophy in life was "Live, Laugh, and Love." She wore a necklace with those words on it.

So, here it was in 1964: the Beatles were the hottest group out there. Well, didn't Mom just get me and my best friend, Neil Winter, tickets for their show at Maple Leaf Gardens! Of course, she wanted to go with us, but as great as mom was, there are some things kids just have to do on their own! Mind you, Mom was so worried we'd get crushed in the crowd, she almost didn't let us go.

And then, there was the famous jazz pianist Oscar Peterson. He wanted to meet Mom. So, they set up a get-together at our house. I wasn't there, but my brother was. Oscar comes in and sits in the living room and Mom brings Steve in to meet him. Now, neither my brother nor I had ever seen a black man before. Not only that, Oscar was very tall. Steve comes in, takes one look at Oscar, and runs out of the room screaming!

You know, it's funny, when I met Oscar years later during a photo shoot, I told him the story and he laughed so hard. He was a wonderful man. I called him the gentle giant. He'd recorded "I'll Never Smile Again" back in 1957 and told me it was one of his favourite songs.

Being around my mom was always cool. In 1964, Ed Sullivan did a show in Toronto from what was then the O'Keefe Centre. Ed asked Mom to come to the show and be in the audience. So, the show runs and Ed's pointing out celebrities in the crowd and, sure enough, he gives her a big shout out. Mom stood up and everyone applauded her, all on live TV. Amazing. Afterwards, we went backstage and met Ed. He wasn't very tall, but that voice and the mannerism was just as you'd expect. Next, Mom took me and my wife, Aline, back to O'Keefe Centre to see the singer Lena Horn. With Mom, it would always be a visit backstage: so, just like before, off we go to meet Lena. Wow! What a fine, beautiful woman. She and Mom had been pals in the old days.

Mom was friends with so many showbiz giants and loved hanging with them. I remember meeting comedian Milton Berle at an after-party held at The Noshery, one of Toronto's great Jewish restaurants.

Of course, I could have met Frank Sinatra a few times, but I didn't really want to. At the time, I thought his music was kind of square—"your parents' music." But I did tell Mom, "If you ever have a chance to meet the Beatles, I will definitely go with you!"

Never happened. Well, not to me anyway. But in 1964, The Beatles were in Nassau filming the movie *Help*. My parents were vacationing there, and, by a stroke of luck, they were all staying at the same hotel. So, I'm at home in Toronto and the mail comes with a big brown envelope addressed to me. I open it and find a photo of the Beatles, signed by each of the Fab Four! John, Paul, George, and Ringo! I just about fainted! I was so overwhelmed. I called Nassau, begging my parents to let me come down so I could meet them. Sadly, my dad said no. I didn't get to go, but I did get an amazing gift! Later on, Mom told me about how she'd connected with the Beatles and how John Lennon told her he loved her music.

Figure 34: Beatles signed photo for Tom

Later in life, Mom became friends with the king of one liners, Henny Youngman. In Miami, he rented an apartment beside her, and I remember spending many days with Henny--he was like a human joke machine! He was playing at the Playboy Club on Collins Avenue and got us tickets for the show. He liked me a lot and, to my surprise, he did a bunch of Tommy Sandler jokes in the show! You know, like, "Tommy Sandler got me tickets once for the Blue Jays' game in Toronto. But they were so high up in the stands, when someone said, 'Oh my God' after a great play, this voice says 'YES?'" Or "Tommy Sandler's a great developer in Canada. He once sold garbage trucks as condos with private elevators!" Henny was always "on," no matter off-stage or on. He once asked me if I'd like to see a photo of his pride and joy. You guessed it: he pulled out a picture of some bottles of Pride furniture polish and Joy dishwasher soap. Only Henny!

Mom used to take me with her to New York City when I was younger: she loved going to Broadway plays and hanging out with music publishers and her old Tin Pan Alley pals. A typical trip included going to a couple of plays and, the next day, we'd head to the jewellers on 47th Street where she'd top up on some bling. Then, we'd hit the Brill Building where she was pals with everyone. She'd even have meetings with the president of MCA Music, an offshoot of the powerful talent agency and television production company.

One time, I was waiting outside the MCA office and this guy comes and sits down beside me. I had written a little folksy type song and thought I was a big famous songwriter. So, we start to talk. He asks me what I've written and the name of the song, and I'm telling him all about it. So, then I ask him what his name is and if he's written anything, thinking I'd show him a thing or two about song writing. Turns out I was sitting beside Bobby Scott who wrote "A Taste of Honey." Yoiks! Guess the apple falls close to the tree: this is shades of Wendy Eisen's story about Mom and Oscar Hammerstein!

So, after she finishes her meeting, I tell the president of MCA that I play guitar and we're hoping to buy a new one while we're in New York. "Hold on," he says, and he grabs the phone and calls the guy who runs Manny's Music, the famous musical instrument store on Music Row (West 48th Street, between 6th and 7th Avenues in Manhattan). "I've got some friends coming by. Take care of them!" Which he did!

After our adventures at the Brill Building, we'd head next door to Dempsey's coffee house and have coffee and cheesecake, "*the*" best cheesecake in the solar system! One time, I sat down, ordered coffee and cheesecake, and there was an elderly guy sitting at the table. Mom knew him quite well and introduced me: turned out to be Johnny Marks, the guy who wrote "Rudolph The Red Nosed Reindeer." Another Yoiks!

Figure 35: Tommy playing guitar

Before we'd leave Dempsey's, Mom would order at least 6 or 7 cheesecakes to go. I couldn't figure out why she bought so many until we got back to Toronto. We're waiting in the customs line. We get closer. Mom's wearing the bling she bought. I'm carrying the Martin guitar we got at Manny's. And our suitcases are full of souvenirs and stuff. We're way over the customs limit on what we're allowed to bring into Canada. Before I know it, Mom's taking a few of the cheesecake boxes and handing them out to the customs agents. My mother is bribing the customs agents with cheesecakes! OMG! I'm going to jail. I kept imagining being in the slammer, with killers and hardened criminals saying, "What're ya in for kid?" What was I gonna say? "For smuggling cheesecakes"? How embarrassing!

Well, needless to say, Mom's ploy worked: the two of us strolled into Canada with not one bag opened by customs. Mom had such charm that not one of the custom guards would say no to her for fear of hurting her feelings. She was such a wonderful schemer in that way. And for me, it was "Life on The Road 101."

One of the other lasting memories I have about Mom is how she adored playing cards, both gin and poker, and she loved to bet on jai alai in Miami, too. She taught me how to bet. I do recall her gambling partner in Miami—a crony of my dad's, who shall remain nameless—let's just say he wasn't exactly a saint. But he loved my mom so much, he'd never asked her to pay back any of her losses (and I'm sure there were a few).

I used to come home from school when I was young. Before I had even opened the front door, I'd hear screaming and laughing. Walking in, smoke would fill the air. I'd head down to the basement where I'd find my mom and at least 12 of her friends in a hot poker game. Dollar bills were stacked up on the table, the girls were smoking, and, as Bonnie Levy explained earlier, most of them were sitting there in their bras! I'll never forget those games or those images! Mom always made me her partner, but only if she won. If she lost, I didn't have to cough up any dough. She was so sweet that way, such a kind person. Thank goodness they weren't drinking. They would have burned the house down!

Being such a fine musician herself, Mom loved all kinds of new music. She thought Lennon and McCartney wrote the best songs and the Rolling Stones had the best name for a group. She was always bugging me to take her along to concerts, but taking your mom wasn't the "cool" thing to do. I felt bad about it because music to her was like breathing.

Of course, she tried to teach me to play the piano. Not the best idea! We had a baby grand Mason & Risch, the piano Mom played every night and day (I still have it today in my home: what memories it brings back). In those days, you could buy pianos with real ivory keys, which ours had. So, there's me, practising and practising, but I hated it: way too boring. So, the creative side of me—always encouraged by Mom—took over and I decided there was an easier way to remember the keys: just carve their name onto the ivory keys themselves. I got a screwdriver and started carving the middle C key. Busted! That's as far as that creative notion got!

Then, there was the time in the 1960s, when the rock scene was happening, and the psychedelic age was upon us. Freedom was in the air, new music, new ideas, and new self-expression were all encouraged. Mom was right there, digging it all! She encouraged me to be creative: so, one day, I went out and bought all these glow-in-the-dark rock posters along with a 3-foot black light. I created mini light shows out of old barbeque motors and Christmas lights. I found out where to buy glow-in-the-dark paint and turned my bedroom into a mind-expanding musical chill environment where one could "relax," as it were.

I learned two things about glow-in-the-dark paint. One: you can over-do it. I mean, I put it *everywhere*: doorknobs, dresser handles, light switches, everywhere! Two: the way this stuff worked was by absorbing light during the day and then letting it glow like crazy at night. Result: when I went to bed and turned off the lights, my room looked like a nuclear bomb had gone off!! Everything was glowing. You needed sunglasses to get to sleep! And if that wasn't enough, I got it on my fingers, so my hands looked like I came from outer space. I could literally read by the light on my hands. And, no surprise, mom *loved* the room. She may not have been quite sure what was going on in there, but she wanted to join us. We didn't think that was such a good idea.

So, we move ahead to my more recent journeys as a photographer where I cross paths with many great artists and musicians. Whenever I meet someone in the music biz, I always share the story of who Mom was and what she wrote. Inevitably, everything stops for a moment, and I get congratulated. And there have been many times when whoever I was shooting would start singing her famous song, like Oscar Peterson, Harry Belafonte, Quincy Jones, Ellis Marsalis... Other public figures and politicians come to mind too, like former Lieutenant Governor of Ontario Lincoln Alexander. At a gala, he held up the entrance to the party while he sang "I'll Never Smile Again" for me. Another memorable moment came while I was shooting a reception with Prince Harry. I was talking to the Irish Ambassador and Colm Wilkinson about my mom and, all of a sudden, the ambassador begins singing the song!

Did you know that the great British pianist George Shearing covered Mom's song in the 1950s? It was an upbeat version, really great. So, imagine my surprise when I was hired to take photos of George, along with Ellis Marsalis, in Toronto for a jazz concert. Later on, I'm checking the shots I'd taken and I'm noticing that in every frame George has his eyes closed. What are the odds of that? Of course, it had never dawned on me that George Shearing was blind!

When I told Ellis about Mom, he was very impressed. So, I asked him, "I guess it was very unusual for a woman to have been involved in the Big Band Era?" I was surprised by his answer: "No. No, it was just the opposite. The music biz was one of the only 'liberal' businesses going: people weren't judged by the colour of their skin, or by their gender, or religious background. They were judged by their ability to play!"

Makes total sense.

Another wonderful celeb I met was Quincy Jones. Q and I came together when I was shooting a gig at the Famous People Players, the non-profit, black light puppetry theatre company that employs people with physical and intellectual disabilities. The organization's founder, my friend, Diane Dupuy, called me and said that apparently Quincy Jones was going to visit the theatre and they wanted to have some photos to mark the occasion. So, I arrive and there he is: *the* Man, Mr. Quincy Delight Jones Jr. (seriously, that's his middle name!). I walk over, introduce myself and tell him, "You may be interested to know that my mom wrote 'I'll Never Smile Again.'" Three things happen. First, his jaw drops. He grabs my hand to shake it, telling me that when he was growing up in the early 1940s, when the song was number one, he knew the story well about how she came to write it. Q then tells me that it was one of the songs that inspired his own career!

Figure 36: Quincy Jones with Tom

But then he adds, "It was one of the best songs ever written!" Then, there's the second thing: he's with this girl, possibly in her late 20s. He leans over to her and says, "There was this young singer named Frank Sinatra..." Well, that's when *my* jaw dropped to the floor! It never occurred to me there would ever be someone who didn't know who Sinatra was! Then, the third thing—this happens after the show—Q gets up on stage to speak, and doesn't he, all of a sudden, say, "I got goose bumps tonight. Once by watching these amazing kids perform. And second, by meeting the son of Ruth Lowe, who wrote one of the greatest songs in music, 'I'll Never Smile Again'" And then, Quincy Jones asks me to stand and take a bow. How cool is that!

My mom's song, and her story, have touched the hearts of so many people around the world. It's still happening today. Mom often told me, "Tommy, the world loves love songs, so write a ballad!" Yeah, right, Mom, like it's that simple!

Figure 37: I'll Never Smile Again in Variety 1958

No mistake about it: mom's music has a timeless quality, touching the lives of so many people, so many generations, so many hearts. Glenn Frey of the Eagles once said, "It's one thing to write music for 'your' time and quite another to write music for 'all' time." This puts Ruth Lowe in a very exclusive category.

And I know we mentioned it earlier, but the fact that she wrote both the words and music for "I'll Never Smile Again" is, in itself, so rare. Look at duos like Rodgers and Hart, Lerner and Lowe, Lennon and McCartney, Elton John and Bernie Taupin, Mick Jagger and Keith Richards... One of the very few other songwriters who crafted both words and music together was the extraordinary Cole Porter. The other was Irving Berlin.

That's the level at which Ruth Lowe played.

Looking back, I definitely inherited my mom's sense of humour and her lust for adventure. And that's what it was like, Growing up Vaudeville.

Yes, no question Tommy was fortunate to grow up as Ruth Lowe's son. But others share equal serendipity simply from being in Ruthie's realm.

Consider this: two fabulous Sinatra stories from one family, neither of which would have occurred without the connection to Ruth Lowe.

"We're talking the early 1990s, as I recall," Sharron Beder is saying. "And I'm at our winter place in Palm Springs, California. My mom and dad, Pearl and Reuben Cappe, are with me and, one evening, we end up going for dinner at Dominick's Restaurant."

Let's pause for a sec to let you know that Dominick's was owned by Dominick Zangari, one of L.A.'s most popular bartenders of the 1970s. It was in Rancho Mirage, one of the nine cities comprising the greater Palm Springs area. The resto eventually becomes Frank Sinatra's favourite dessert locale to watch *Monday Night Football*. In fact, when U2's Bono comes to town to shoot a video of "I've Got You Under My Skin" for Sinatra's smash 1993 album, *Duets*, they shoot it at Dominick's.

Back to Sharron's story. "There's a Coachella Valley pipeline that tells Sinatra worshipers where he'll be, but no one has tipped us off this evening. So, the three of us are just there, having a wonderful dinner, and that's just fine. And the time comes to go. Dad leaves to pay the bill and get the car. But as Mom and I are standing up, I look over and there's this huge black man walking into the place. I mean, he was big enough that you definitely turned your head. He immediately goes to the bar along with the guy behind him, who's wearing a snap-brimmed fedora. The guy takes off the hat, places it on the bar, and orders a drink. I almost fainted: it's Frank Sinatra.

"Now, I was a fan of Ole Blue Eyes, but my mom was an original bobby-soxer. No one was bigger than Frank Sinatra to Pearl Cappe! So, I say to her, 'Mom, there he is. Your idol. We have to go over and talk to him.' Well, I thought Mom was going to pass out. 'Talk to him!' she says. 'You want me to go over and talk to Frank Sinatra!? Not happening!'"

"I have to tell you, I have no fear when it comes to that kind of thing," Sharron says. "You're looking at the gal who walked over out of nowhere at the Toronto Film Festival and wished Dustin Hoffman '*Shannah tovah*', you know, have a happy, healthy new year. He says back to me, '*Shannah tovah* to you and your family'. Anyway, I'm pleading with Mom, 'You can't pass up this opportunity! You're his biggest fan.' So, I eventually convince her. But she says, 'Let me visit the bathroom first,' and off she goes.

"Now, I have to tell you, my mom was a very good-looking lady back then. Still is for that matter, at age 95. So, I knew that even if she had nothing to say, Sinatra would give her the time of day, knowing how he appreciated beautiful women.

"Well, I wait. And I wait. She's not coming out of that bathroom. So, what do I do? I get up and walk right over to the bar, intent on stalling time with Frank Sinatra until Mom shows up. But, as I get near, an immense arm goes up, blocking my way. It belongs to the huge gentlemen I referred to earlier, obviously Mr. Sinatra's bodyguard. But again, with me, we're talking about a take-no-prisoners kind of person, so I say to him, in a voice loud enough that I know Sinatra can hear, 'I just want to greet Mr. Sinatra on behalf of my mother-in-law who was best friends with Ruth Lowe.'"

"That works big time! Sinatra wheels around. He says 'Let her by' to the big guy. He lowers his arm and invites me into 'the presence.' 'Hi, I'm Frank,' Sinatra says. 'What were you saying about Ruth Lowe?' And for the next 10 minutes or so, I'm regaling him with stories about Ruthie and Toronto and those crazy poker parties and everything. And Sinatra's loving it. We end up talking about kids and I don't know what all."

"But I'm worried that Mom's missing out on this.

"'Frank, give me a moment,' I say. 'I have to get my mom. She's such a fan of yours.' And I walk off to the ladies' room. But when I enter, there's no one there. What the heck? Then, I see it: there's a small door that, when I open it, goes to the lobby and the front door of Dominick's. Mom obviously got cold feet and vamoosed!

"So, I return to where Frank's waiting at the bar and say, 'I'm really sorry but my mother's taken a flyer on you.' He laughs. And to his credit, he asks her name, grabs a napkin, writes on it, 'Pearl, sorry I missed you, Frank S.' and says, 'Give her this.'"

"And, you know, I didn't talk to her for two days after that: how could she let an opportunity like this go by? To this day, she still admits it was a very big mistake!"

The clock moves up to 2013. Bobby Beder, Sharron's husband, is at their place in Palm Desert. "I heard there was a big charity event to be held at a local person's home," he says. "And the news was that Frank Sinatra's kids, Nancy, Tina, and Frank Jr., were to be there. Now, just like Sharron's mom, I have to say I'm a huge Frank Sinatra fan. Love his music. There is no better. My favourite entertainer. A genius. In fact, on December 12th, his birthday, I always head over to Desert Memorial Park in Cathedral City." This is the cemetery where this most enduring of all 20th century American entertainers is, beside his parents, Marty and

Dolly Sinatra, and his Uncle Vincent Mazzola, who had lived with the Sinatras since Frank was a teen in Hoboken, and Sinatra's last best friend, Jilly Rizzo. It's interesting that the Sinatra gravestone is marked simply, "Beloved husband & father" and "The Best Is Yet To Come," the title of that 1964 standard by Carolyn Leigh and Cy Coleman. Here, he is buried with a bunch of sentimental items packed for him on this journey by his family: cherry Lifesavers, Tootsie Rolls, a pack of Camels, a Zippo lighter, stuffed animals, a dog biscuit, a bottle of Jack Daniels, and the 10 dimes he always carried in his coat in case he needed to make a phone call.

"So, there's going to be this fundraiser for a branch of the Desert Museum that's opening up," Bobby continues, "and I figure, I never got to meet Frank but maybe I can meet one of the kids. So, I buy a ticket and I attend the reception at this beautiful home. Couple of hundred people there and I don't know a soul, of course, but I mingle around and suddenly I see Nancy Sinatra over in a corner, more or less by herself. I figure, 'OK Bobby, here's your chance.' I amble over, but I hesitate because you can tell she's not overly inviting. Anyway, I screw up my courage and kind of blurt out, "Hi, I'm Bobby Beder from Toronto and you don't know me but one of my mother Jean's best friends was Ruth Lowe and…' Well, I never got further than that. Nancy absolutely lights up at the mention of Ruthie's name. She tells me about meeting Tommy a few years ago, and I explain how our parents were best friends, that Mom and Ruth were so close and always played in those crazy poker games and that my dad, Monte, was Nat's partner in N.L Sandler and Company, where I worked myself. And we have this amazing, wonderful conversation for about 20 minutes, Nancy and me. And it was the mention of Ruth's name that opened that door. Even later that evening, every time I see her, Nancy calls out through the crowd, 'Hi Bobby, how are you?' like we're old best friends. It was quite amazing. Really special. And all thanks to Ruth."

Chapter Thirteen

Sandler's Way

No question at all, Nat Sandler was a hard-nosed conservative businessman. He certainly wasn't a creative person.

"Actually, down deep, I think my mom kind of intimidated him," suggests Tom Sandler. "He was an impressive guy, my dad, no question, really knew his way around any kind of business deal. But creativity wasn't his thing, and I think it scared him. He didn't get it. And Mom was so creative in so many ways. I'm sure he felt spooked by that. In fact, he was behind my mom nixing a possible MGM biopic about her life: she would have been played by Judy Garland. I really don't think he wanted that kind of exposure for his family."

"But let's not sell him short," says Cookie Sandler. "I mean, c'mon, we're talking about a guy who re-launched Toronto's first nightclub, the Club One-Two. And we're talking about a guy who'd always squeeze fresh orange juice for everybody each morning at the cottage. I loved Nat. Yes, he was conservative. And sure, he didn't have Ruth's free spirit. But they loved each other and made a great couple. And I loved him: he was a great father-in-law."

"Dad was a terrific promoter," says Tom. "At one time, in the late 1950s, he owned the trains that carried people around the Canadian National Exhibition. It was pretty cool. What impressed me the most was that Dad had a parking pass that allowed him to drive his car right onto the grounds at the CNE and park there for free. That was totally rad!

"It was there that I got my first summer job. I played a werewolf at the Haunted Mansion. Great gig: I chased the girls around a lot (but I never bit any). I too got a parking pass for the grounds: the circle was completed. OK, I only made a buck an hour and worked 15-hour double shifts some days... but it was *amazing*!

"Dad also got me my first full-time job. He was friends with so many people, so he just calls up his pal, Harry Solomon, who ran—wait for it—the Exquisite Form Brassiere Company. Harry was a great guy and hired me to work full time in his factory making bras. And all this time, I didn't think my dad had a sense of humour!

"Pardon the pun, but life was *full*: music on one side, business opportunities on the other. What more could a guy like me ask for?"

"My memory of Nat is that he was pretty stern," says Lynda Rapp. "Not the life of the party. But he was a really good dad, a good grandpa, and he loved his wife. And, you know, I can't imagine being married to someone who wrote a song called 'I'll Never Smile Again,' and it's got nothing to do with you at all! He was a little more laid back while she was the rambunctious one. But they were a love affair for sure."

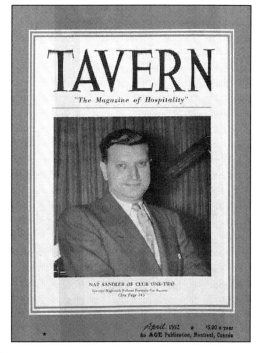

Figure 38: Nat Sandler in Tavern Magazine

Nat loved doing deals. He was like the Godfather, but without the bullets. He had a beautiful wife, who was a celebrity. He had two sons, who were good kids. He was respected, compassionate. But he'd grown up with an edge to him, his own father having been a real Russian tyrant. Still, for all the pluck, he was, in reality, quite a shy man who preferred staying under the radar while his wife soared high.

For her part, Ruth needed the structure that Nat could bring to their life. She liked tough guys. She liked a man to be a real man (think Sinatra; think Dorsey). It was a romantic kind of thing. Nat wasn't one to back down or run from anything, and she had a lot of respect for him. She knew she had a pretty forceful personality, but she didn't want a guy who would have to hang on her reputation to make a life of his own.

"My dad was crazy about my mom, that much I know," says Tommy. "I mean, he'd grown up in a pretty conservative style. So, there you have my mom, the social butterfly whose free and spontaneous, and then you have Dad who's very down to earth and grounded. He kept the trains running: whereas my mom would be the one playing on the train! But seriously, they lived a really good life. My mom respected my dad, thought the world of him. I'm not sure Dad ever understood how important Mom's music was. He was locked into the male-as-the-provider role with a strong personality."

"I worked downtown so I used to drive up to the cottage with him," says Cookie. "It was kind of uncomfortable at first. But we started talking about how he and Ruth had met and stuff like that and before long, it became very easygoing. He'd tell me about parts of his life I knew nothing about, like when he was managing Casa Loma, the famous mansion in Toronto. He was really good to me. He and Ruthie would take me and Steve places. It was really fun."

Cookie stops for a moment, lost in thought. A smile crosses her face.

"Here's a funny story about Nat," she says. "He was a founding member of Oakdale, a Jewish golf club. But once he and Ruth bought the property on Lake Simcoe and it became apparent that they'd be spending a fair amount of time there, Ruthie says, 'Nat, forget it. You can't spend all your life golfing if I'm going to be up here at the cottage.' So, doesn't Nat just give up golf. Just like that. Never golfed again. Literally. But here's what's funny. Later on, Ruthie goes out and joins Orchard Beach, the only Jewish golf club near the cottage. So, she ends up playing golf all the time and Nat goes fishing, his new pastime."

Cookie recalls that when Ruth first got sick with cancer, Nat stopped everything to look after her.

"After she died, my father-in-law and I stayed close," she says. "Nat and I would go to movies together. My friends thought it was weird going to a movie with your father-in-law, but we enjoyed our time together. I used to say it took two Sandler men to keep me happy!"

"He was a good man," says Tommy. "He was a real promoter. A real doer. An entrepreneur. And a charitable person raising money for Variety Club and B'nai B'rith and others. You know, from whisky funds in Scotland to gold mines in Costa Rica, he was a very smart businessman. Actually, I tried to work with him, but I was too much of a free-spirited teenager. Steve was able to do that, but I'm more of a romantic guy than a businessman."

And then, there's this from retired Canadian businessman, investor, author, and philanthropist Seymour Schulich:[19]

"Most of the time that I knew the family, we were in Montreal, and Nat was up here in Toronto," he says. "We worked out an arrangement with Ned Goodman and myself: we were both partners in Beutel, Goodman and Co. for 22 years. Once a month, we'd

Figure 39: Seymour Schulich
Photo: National Post

come to Toronto and spend an hour talking to the stockbrokers. That's when we got to know Nat. He was a securities salesman,

---

[19] Photo republished with the express permission of: National Post, a division of Postmedia Network, Inc

very cheerful, very likeable man. He was older than us, and I had the greatest respect for him.

"He had a lot of financial experience and he would share his expertise with you, and he was just an enjoyable guy, fun to visit. You looked forward to visiting the guy. Very positive. A character, a successful salesman.

"Here's a Nat Sandler story you'll love," says Seymour. "I was pitching—maybe a little too verbose. And he stops me and says something that stuck with me for my whole life. He said, 'Seymour, once you've made the sale, stop selling.' It's really...it's remarkable how you'll bring people around and you've made the sale, but you keep talking and you start creating doubts in their mind. It happens quite a bit. I was never a marketing guy: I've got one skill in life, which is the ability to pick stocks that go up. It's a very good skill, and if you can do that, you can get up and pee on people's desks. But Nat's advice stuck with me my whole life. Often, I go into retail stores and I'm sold on something and the guy just keeps on blabbing away, and I say, 'My friend, let me give you a piece of valuable advice: once you've made the sale, stop selling!'

"Nat was always a fellow we were closely aligned with. We liked him. I think we did the very first underwriting I completed for a company called Pinot Petroleum and I think Nat raised almost two million dollars. He was one of three underwriters that participated in the deal. He was a class act.

"On a personal level, I went to their country house a couple of times, on the east side of Lake Simcoe. It was very nice. The kids were there, Stephen and Tommy. I knew Steve better because he worked with his dad. And everyone knew that Ruth had written Sinatra's theme song and we thought it was great but we, you know, we certainly never thought a lot about it one way or the other. Never realized she was getting a lot of royalty money, not something we really knew about or thought about much."

At the end of the day, Seymour Schulich feels what defined Ruth and Nat was that they were a class act. "If there was a word to describe Nat Sandler, and both of them as a couple: they were very classy people. And I'm not saying that to be flattering or anything else: they really were a class act, and I always enjoyed the time I spent with both of them. Down to earth people, very much so. Self-made man. Brokerage firm was small: he took on deals that establishment guys wouldn't take on. And Ruth: let me tell you something, no one ever talked about her songs. It wasn't an area of particular interest to anyone in our business, so they never belaboured that.

"I do know Ruth came from no money. Her dad died penniless. Nat's financial background? Don't know. My view is that he was part of a small brokerage firm, so they had to take more of a speculative deal. But I loved the guy, he always made you feel good."

Seymour smiles to himself, then offers this:

"You know, there are two things I've learned in life as I've gotten older that are very important. The first is that the only thing you can control in life is your own behaviour. Don't try to control your wife or your kids or employees: it's very difficult, and they'll get aggravated. Stop doing that. I used to do that but don't do it anymore. The second thing I learned in life is this: people forget what you say. People forget what you do. But no one will ever forget the way you made them feel. If I had a deficiency, it was that I didn't suffer fools gladly in the old days. But Nat was always a classy guy, a guy who you always felt good seeing. He always had a smile on his face. He was always interested in your situation, your problems. He recognized us coming up: young Jewish boys trying to learn the ropes. Nat was a father figure to some extent. He would have been an integral part of the Toronto establishment then. A real class act."

Out of nowhere, Seymour looks up, winks, then adds, "By the way, did I tell you that my daughter's got a PhD? Yup. Poppa has dough!"

Chapter Fourteen

Why Not A Nightclub?

"You know, for all that's been said about my dad being a serious-minded, single-focused businessman, there is the story of the Club One-Two," says Tommy Sandler. "He took chances, wasn't afraid to take a shot at things.

"As I recall, the story of how Dad bought the club goes like this. It's Rosh Hashanah, the Jewish holiday, and Dad and his pal, Lou Chestler, are attending the service at their synagogue. The rabbi's just about to go into a sermon but Dad and his buddy are getting a little bored. They decide, with another friend of theirs, to cut out, enjoy a couple of drinks, and talk over the potential for the next great developments in their lives. So, they sneak out and head over to the other guy's house. A bottle of scotch is uncorked, and they snort back a few shots. Well, one thing leads to another and the three of them have a fine old time with several more shots.

"Next day, my dad, somewhat worse for wear from the previous day's exploits, has a haunting feeling he can't explain. Suddenly, the light goes on. He calls Lou right away. 'We didn't agree to buy a night club yesterday, did we?' he asks. Sure enough, they had! *That* was the beginning of the notorious Club One-Two."

Seems the boys, thoroughly enjoying their revelry, had somehow become aware that a lounge in downtown Toronto was for sale. It was originally called The Club Norman (presumably named after the owner, Norm Cornell) and boasted the address #12 Adelaide East. Aided by lots of fine scotch, Nat and his pals had ended up as the new owners of what was Toronto's first nightclub.

Records show that the newly decorated nightspot opened under Nat Sandler's direction on March 24, 1951. Ruth helped sequester the Irving Fields Trio as the opening attraction. And why Irving Fields, you ask? Simple. Born Yitzhak Schwartz, in New York City, Irving became a pianist and lounge music artist who, with his trio, was famous for their album *Bagels & Bongos.* You don't recognize this Decca Records hit? Why, it sold over two million copies!

The menu of the day featured a bottle of Bright's President Champagne for $7 and a shot of booze for seventy cents. There was, of course, a cover charge of $1, but on the weekends that escalated to a buck fifty. And they were proud to say that Club One-Two was the only Ontario member of the Diners' Club of America.

At one point, the nightclub had been run by Tommy Holmes, known as "the Toots Shor of Canada"—that comparison being with Bernard "Toots" Shor, best known as the proprietor of the legendary saloon and restaurant, Toots Shor's Restaurant, in Manhattan. Toots was celebrated as a saloonkeeper, friend, and confidant to some of New York's biggest celebrities. Holmes worked for a while with Nat too.

Mike Filey, well-known Canadian historian and journalist, has shared that the Club One-Two promo brochure from the 1950s presented Nat Sandler as one of the "affable" owners of the nightspot who was "looking to help people have a good time in Toronto." The piece goes on to say, "*Cherchez la femme*, and you'll find Mrs. Sandler, a celebrity in her own right. Blond, with deep-set eyes, she is the former Ruth Lowe, composer of the long-time

Figure 40: Ruth and Nat 1963

favorite 'I'll Never Smile Again,' and many other popular songs. Mrs. Sandler puts her talent to work in auditioning the entertainers, usually in New York, with Nat giving the final nod. As a result of this expert screening, only the cream of New York TV and stage talent is heard from the small revolving stage."

The Club One-Two was on the cusp of a new age, emerging from the post-World War II era. Toronto was becoming a city that was both mysterious and alluring. And who better than Nat Sandler to lead the way to sophistication as the proprietor of a fancy nightspot where the elite meet to greet.

Figure 41: Club One-Two Opening Night Invitation

"It was kind of like Rick's Cafe in Casablanca," says Tommy. "At that time, it was the first and only nightclub in Toronto. You'd get everyone in the city going there, from the police chief on down. And Mom would use her connections and help get the talent who performed at the Club. Don't forget, she'd managed the Murray Room night club in New York back in the 40s. So, she booked Steve Lawrence and Eydie Gormé, who first appeared together there. They always sang Mom's song in their Vegas act right up until Eydie passed away. And Mom actually helped famed comedy duo Wayne & Shuster get started. It was a ritzy place too—tuxedos, the whole nine yards. My dad had managed a hotel up in Bala, Muskoka, so he had *some* experience with this kind of thing.

Figure 42: Club One-Two brochure
Courtesy of Mike Filey

"And, of course, this was before he got into the stock promotion business."

Oh, and about that Wayne & Shuster reference... An early break had come during the college days enjoyed by Johnny Wayne and Frank Shuster when Ruth Lowe recommended them to a friend of hers at a talent agency. And so, began their legendary rise.

"Actually," Johnny Wayne would recall later with a smile, "we don't know why Ruth was so enthusiastic. I don't think she thought we were that funny because she wrote 'I'll Never Smile Again' after catching our act!"

But funny they were and would go on to be Ed Sullivan's most frequently recurring guests on his famed television variety show, appearing 67 times. Despite suggestions they could relocate to the U.S. where their act would gain even more ground, Johnny and Frank chose to remain in Canada, staying in the land where Ruth Lowe had given them that first important shot that they needed to take off and soar.

Chapter Fifteen

Put Your Dreams Away

It was the early 1970s.

Ruth had begun complaining of internal pain.

This was the outset of a 10-year struggle with cancer.

It was a fight that would test the vibrant, gentle woman like never before.

"It was shocking," says Tommy. "You felt so helpless. It was ongoing for so many years. She'd get better, then she'd get worse. My dad just did what the doctors told them to do. Everyone thought it would go away and she'd be fine. It didn't really hit home until the end.

"You got used to her being ill," he continues. "Eventually, it was like a mixed blessing because she was suffering, and you didn't want to see that continue. She looked horrible at the end, dealing with pain. She just wasn't herself anymore."

Bonnie Levy's voice takes on a conspiratorial whisper. "I don't know if you should write this or not but when Ruth was so sick and dealing with increasing pain, I got her some marijuana to help subside her suffering. Now, this is 1980—a long time ago. But I 'had a friend who had a friend' and could get their hands on some grass. It was *verboten* at that time, but I managed to obtain some and got it to Ruth and she so appreciated that. It really helped her deal with the sickness."

Bonnie then reveals that she found Ruth to be uncharacteristically sad towards the end.

"Here was this lady who'd been so up, so cheerful, life of the party, so concerned about everyone else: but now, she had just become sad at the end. I don't remember any joy at all. It was mostly, just sad..."

Ruth Lowe died on a snowy day in January.

The 4th.

It was 1981.

She was 66 years old.

Nat contacted Stuart Rosenberg. The retired rabbi, a spiritual leader of Canada's Jews and an author himself, had led the Beth Tzedec synagogue in Toronto, the largest Conservative congregation in Canada. He had officiated at important Sandler family events in the past, such as Steve's and Tommy's bar mitzvahs.

The bereaved husband knew there would be no one else who could lead the gathering of family and close friends at Ruth's very personal, very intimate funeral.

"Fortunately for us all, she did smile again," commented Rabbi Rosenberg in his touching obituary on that sad day. "She laughed again, she danced again, she sang again, and made us sing with her. For all of us, here in this room, and in many other places across the world, wherever music is enjoyed and a deeply felt emotion, warmly received and wanton, she smiles now. We are reminded of the great struggle of life in which she was engaged: life itself made her sing in the midst of her crying, turning lament into praise. Ruthie was beautiful within and beautiful without. There are days within any man or woman where we say, 'I will never smile again.' I'm sure that this is one such day for many of us. And yet, she made us smile again. She made us live again. She made us see again. I think of Ruthie as one who gave back something to the world, when something was taken from her. She gave herself back to the world. She smiled again."

The rabbi went on to comment on the fusion of joy and spirit Ruth stood for in her life. The relishing of the unexpected. The feeling that there was never a dull moment.

"She will be remembered long after we are gone," he concluded. "But remember *yourself* in her presence. Remember what she did for you. And me. And all those who touched her life, and whose lives she touched. Remember yourself as Ruthie's friend."

"It was a big funeral, a big deal," recalls Lynda Rapp. "Ruthie had a lot of friends. She was well-known, not just for her music but for her work in the community and all the fun she had with those poker games and everything. And the kids' friends all came too. It was a big event."

Tommy wipes away a tear. "I have such wonderful memories," he says. "I mean, as a kid, eating cheesecake in New York with Johnny Marks, my mom's friend. Spending time with Duke Ellington, Ella Fitzgerald, Ed Sullivan, Lena Horne, Bobby Scott...so many amazing people who were always in her realm. And then...then, she was gone..."

In retrospect, Tom thinks his mom had more great songs inside her. But she had become tied to a new lifestyle: a family and different values to which she decided to dedicate herself. Trying to write a hit song and get it out there is a huge amount of work. Are you going to do that? Or raise a family?

Having lost her father and then her husband so early in her life... she never talked about this to her sons.

"I don't think she wanted us to be traumatized by that," says Tom. "But where it became apparent was when she sat down and played the piano. She hit depths of pain and sorrow. You couldn't help but understand. Still, she never verbalized it. It came out in the music. She wanted to protect herself and protect us from what had happened, I think.

"And there were times when she missed being closer to the music scene and being more involved in it," he continues. "But she had a tremendous lifestyle: amazing house, fantastic cottage, great place in Florida. Tons of friends. So, it helped balance things out. But you could hear it in her playing, this longing. And she was always calling New York or Chicago. She'd call Sammy Cahn or the head of a big music company just to chat, you know, to keep in the game."

Ruth even asked her son to write a song with her.

"She loved gospel," laughs Tom. "So, we wrote a gospel tune together. 'Take Your Sins to the River.' It was great fun. Mom had a debut party at the house, and she got the Travellers to release it. They were best known for their rendition of the Canadian version of 'This Land Is Your Land,' so it was a big deal.

"She was so well-loved: so good natured and generous—and a star. Very encouraging to anyone and everyone.

"You know, looking back, it would be wrong to confine Mom's creativity just to music. I mean, we're talking a lady who loved cooking, needlepointing, knitting, and so much more. I remember her taking forever to needlepoint an Aztec Sun God. Now, we're not talking about a little doily-like kind of thing: this was 4' x 4'! And if that wasn't enough, she went on to do a needlepointed Buddha the same size. Mom was never one for half measures!

"One year, she knitted all of us great wool winter jackets. I'll never forget it: mine had racing cars. And then, there was the time she had all this different coloured wool left over from her various projects. So, she decides to knit a coat: a coat of many colours, like Joseph's in the Bible. Things were going along great until she realized she didn't have enough wool to finish the jacket. So, out she goes to buy more wool. And you guessed it: having finished the jacket, she now had wool left over! What next?"

There's also the matter of the black cardigan sweaters. Ruth truly had a caring, affectionate soul and, whenever anyone did something nice for her, darned if she wouldn't send them a black cardigan sweater from out of nowhere, just to acknowledge their kindness. Even Ralph Edwards, famed host of the *This Is Your Life* TV show on which Ruth appeared, received a sweater.

"When Mom died," recalls Tom, "columnist Gary Lautens wrote a really nice story about her in the Toronto Star. What came to mind for him was, after his first interview with her, a package arrived. Inside: a black cardigan sweater! He ended his tribute to Mom's death by saying. 'I think I'll put on that sweater, have a scotch, and listen to 'I'll Never Smile Again.'"

When Ruth Lowe passed away, her family was left with all of her music, manuscripts, photos, letters, and scrapbooks.

"We discovered that she'd even kept all her music contracts with publishers," says Tom. "Going through it was like walking through an historic gold mine. It was then that I realized I had the original recording of Percy Faith's first version of "I'll Never Smile Again" on a 78 rpm disc, from 1939. When I saw it, and held it, it was like I had uncovered something rare and priceless.

"Mom was smart to keep everything. In the collection of artefacts was the original contract she had with the Dorsey Brothers. There was also a contract with Walter Kent, who wrote among other songs, 'The White Cliffs of Dover.' Mom and Walter performed together, playing two pianos on stage. Dame Vera Lynn (who died in 2020 at 102 years of age) made 'The White Cliffs of Dover' famous, of course. But did you know that she also recorded 'I'll Never Smile Again' and Mom's second huge hit, 'Put Your Dreams Away'"?

Figure 43: Ruth with Walter Kent

They found boxes of 78s, all by different artists who covered her most famous song. Stars like Billie Holiday, Fats Waller,

Django Reinhardt, Les Paul, Count Basie, Oscar Peterson, Dave Brubeck, George Shearing, Tommy Dorsey, Eydie Gormé, Joe Williams, The Platters (who did a slam dunk version), Bobby Vinton—hundreds, literally.

Figure 44: Saint Louis Blues

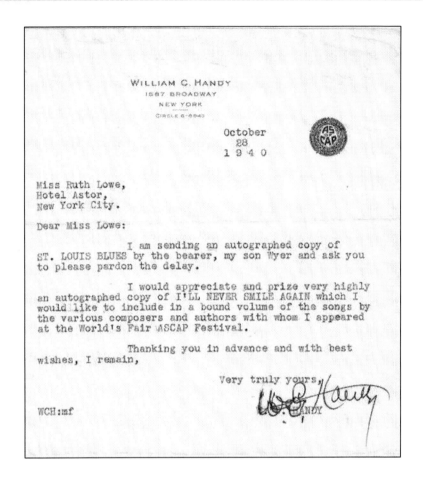

Figure 45: William Handy letter about St. Louis Blues

"I also discovered a 78 that was recorded by Louis Armstrong," says Tom. "It's Louis singing Happy Birthday to Bing Crosby. My mom partied with the best!"

"And then, there were the telegrams—wires from the likes of Tommy Dorsey, inviting her to his new office opening on Broadway; Toots Shore; Milton Berle—and a copy of the 'St Louis Blues' signed by the song's composer, W.C. Handy, the father of American Blues. Along with his autograph on the sheet music, there was a letter from W.C. to Mom, asking if they could exchange autographs! Turns out, Mom and W.C. met in New York at a songwriter's convention. In the letter he said he'd send his son back to New York to exchange the autographed music because he was living in New Orleans at the time. This was an enormous honour: my mom was now not only hanging with the greats: she *was* one of the greats!

"Amazing, isn't it: a single, widowed, Jewish, Canadian girl had blown the lid off the music industry worldwide. Ruth Lowe was now one of the architects of the American ballad!"

And even today, almost 40 years after her death, surprises continue to evolve. Tom recently received a link to a 1941 Columbia Pictures featurette starring none other than The Three Stooges, it's title: "I'll Never Heil Again," capitalizing on the incredible notoriety of Ruth's song. Production notes state "the film's title is a parody of song title 'I'll Never Smile Again,' written by Ruth Lowe and released in 1940 by Tommy Dorsey and his Orchestra featuring vocals by Frank Sinatra with the Pied Pipers. The song reached No. 1 on Billboard for 12 weeks."

As they say, when you're sent up by the Stooges, you've really arrived!

And there's this, from the same "strange but true" trove of arcane musical tidbits, this time dealing with a copycat. Seems a guy from Brooklyn named Rocco started making the rounds in 1940, telling the world that *he'd* sold "I'll Never Smile Again" to Tommy Dorsey. In a newspaper article, Ruth—described as a "Key Kitten"—says that "Rocco's gonna get a socko" as she and Dorsey laugh off the intruder.

After Ruth's death, Nat Sandler had to pick up his life.

"My dad just kept going after she died," says Stephen. "He was trying to figure out where to go and what to do from there. Cookie was great with him."

Howard and Ruthie Himel had been the Sandler's best friends, but Howard too had died. So, Nat and Ruthie—funny about the same name—got together and traveled a bit and hung out together.

"They kept each other company," says Steve. "But each of them kept their own homes."

Nat died in 1991 at the age of 84, the result of a heart attack he suffered while in Florida.

The end of an era had taken place.

Chapter Sixteen

Onwards

Bringing up kids is never an easy task. But when we start insisting that they commemorate the lives of past family members, it can put pressure on adolescents to play a game in which perhaps only the parents see value.

So, what do you do when you have a famous relative? Especially given the fact that her grandchildren were pretty young at the time of her death.

Figure 46: The Sandlers at Lake Simcoe

For Stephen and Cookie Sandler, and Tom and Aline Sandler, they've elected to take the attitude that Gramma Ruth is someone worth knowing. It's all about balance. And it's paid off.

To begin with, each of the current generation of Sandlers knows who their grandmother was, and each recognizes her amazing contribution to the Great American Songbook. So do their friends.

"All my close friends know what she did for popular music," says Robin Sandler, Tom and Aline's son.

Robin realizes it's a great honour to be the grandchild of Ruth Lowe. "It's an amazing thing knowing that a young Canadian and Jewish woman, who also happened to be my grandmother, helped launch the career of the greatest singer in the history of music," he says. "To have turned the tragedy of losing her husband into a song that became the anthem for her generation is pretty inspiring. And it's kind of special to be her grandchild. It's rare to be related to someone who wrote one of the greatest and most influential songs of the 20th century. Even today, Ol' Blue Eyes is known as the greatest singer that ever was and ever will be. And everyone who came after him owes a lot to him and his singing style. And to think: my grandmother put him on the map!"

"She was extremely affectionate," comments Scott Sandler, Steve and Cookie's son. "I remember her voice singing to me and sitting beside her on the piano bench. And I have memories of driving in the car with her and Papa Nat in Miami. I remember waiting for her to wake up in the mornings at the cottage, and her being the first person I wanted to see."

Asked about whether Ruth's famous songs resonate with him, Scott says, "Of course, I like them. They are great songs. And she is also my grandmother. It makes me feel special that she left a legacy. In doing so, she has instilled a love of music in my family that is passing down through the generations. I think that's pretty special."

Speaking of that love of music, you have to wonder if the music gene with which Ruth was blessed can travel across the line?

"I love music," says Scott. "We play lots of songs in our house and dance with our kids just as I did with my parents growing up. My brother Anthony, Cousin Robin, and I all play instruments, and my kids are learning to play as well."

"I do like to consider myself musical," says Robin. "I play guitar and piano and have always loved music since I was born. I have no doubt that my grandmother was a huge part in my love of music. I don't think I would be as passionate about music if I was someone else's grandchild."

"I remember her being happy, kind, and loving," recalls Michael Plotnick, Aline's son from her previous marriage, Tom's stepson. "I know about her entire career. And although it's not the music I listen to today, there is a sense of timelessness to her songs. She was a woman ahead of her times, able to accomplish something truly rare and unbelievable."

Asked about Ruth's legacy, Michael says, "I think hers is a great story and inspirational for young Canadian artists, both writers and musicians. I feel special and honored to have had such a famous grandmother."

Anthony Sandler, Steve and Cookie's other son, is convinced Ruth was a woman ahead of her times. "She was able to accomplish something truly rare and unbelievable," he says.

Robin Sandler: "I think every generation should learn about what my grandmother did and how she helped shape the course of popular music. She was way ahead of her time and her story should be seen as an inspiration to all musicians. It's a long time coming and it's an important story, not only for the history of music but for Canada as well."

And then there's this from Scott Sandler, sharing a bitter/sweet memory from his youth.

"When she was getting sick, I had a birthday party in Toronto, and she wasn't there. She had sent a tape recorder as a gift and in it was a cassette with her singing to me and telling me she loved me. How cool is that! But I had never used a tape recorder and accidentally erased the cassette. I thought my mother was going to kill me! I have always regretted not having that recording.

But the funny thing is I can still remember her voice on it perfectly. It makes me both sad and happy to think about it. It was so long ago, and I was so young...but I still feel like I miss her all the time."

And then there's this: the memories never stop.

Toronto's *Globe & Mail* newspaper runs an article featuring "A 'Healing' Return to the Home of Songwriter Ruth Lowe." Tom Sandler attends with a reporter to walk through the house where he grew up. The recollections come flooding back. Here are some segments from the article...

> *When I was younger, she had—oh God, this is bringing back some memories…* "Tom Sandler *stops mid-word as his voice cracks.* "She had bought me a record player," *he resumes, scanning his former childhood bedroom.* "It was in the shape of a jukebox and it would glow. And my first record was a baseball record with Dizzy Dean or something like that, then Honeycomb by Jimmie Rodgers.*
>
> *It's likely Mr. Sandler's mother, Ruth Lowe (1914-1981), brought that record home for her tow-headed, rambunctious son in the early autumn of 1957, after it had hit No. 1 on the Billboard chart. Of course Ms. Lowe knew a winner when she heard one: 17 years before, her masterful "I'll Never Smile Again," as performed by Tommy Dorsey and His Orchestra and crooned by a fresh-faced Frankie Sinatra, reached No. 1 in July and stayed there until October.*
>
> *In the fall of 1957, the Sandler-Lowe family had been living in their ranch-style home in Toronto, just north of Eglinton and Bathurst, for less than a year. They'd come from Chiltern Hill Road, a street just south of that same*

intersection. Mr. Sandler, then seven-years-old, remembers staying at his aunt and uncle's house for the weekend, then his uncle driving him 'home' to an unfamiliar place. It would become very familiar, since young Tommy—who was named after Dorsey—wouldn't leave until his parents sold the place in early 1973.

Today, Mr. Sandler, an accomplished photographer, is standing with the son of the couple who bought the place, Lawrence Cohen, who, ironically, was given the same bedroom when his family moved in, and his wife of 39 years, Judi Cohen. Mr. Cohen, a real estate lawyer, and Ms. Cohen, a travel professional, moved into the house in 2000 after Mr. Cohen's father passed away, and they're listening, rapt, to Mr. Sandler's reminiscences.

Indeed, when the Cohen family bought the house, Ms. Lowe's enormous, mono Wharfedale speaker was right where she'd left it. A third memory is that she had a "trippy" way with interior decorating, with rugs-upon-rugs, banana-shaped cushions in the basement rec room, lots of color, "artsy" cork-ball drapes in the kitchen, and paintings on practically every wall. "She was not boring," he admits. "I don't know if it's because she came from such poverty, but she was having fun.

"It was a great house for parties," Tom Sandler remembers. "My mom was incredible, she had the whole house wired for speakers— way before stereo, this was high fidelity!"

*"It's very healing being here," finishes Mr.
Sandler, smiling. "I think Mom would be very
happy."*[20]

Neat article. But the story doesn't end there. Have a look at
this email that came to Tom the day the item ran:

Dear Tom:
*It was so wonderful to read the article in the
Globe today about you presenting a framed
photograph of your Mom's (Ruth Lowe) copy of
"I'll Never Smile Again" to the current owners of
your family home in the 50's. It is a piece of
music I have loved for years and I will tell you
why.*
*My Dad was stationed on the Queen
Charlotte Islands (Haida Gwaii) during World
War II as Recreation director for the RCAF base
of Alliford Bay. It was his job to keep morale up
by entertaining the personnel with activities and
music. He played the piano, but copies of
popular music were not readily available, so Dad
taught himself to play by ear. "I'll Never Smile
Again" was a favorite!!!*
*Back home in Ontario in the later Forties and
Fifties, my Dad was regularly at the piano in our
home, Woodstock Radio Station (What's Behind
the Green Door) Program, and community
functions playing "I'll Never Smile Again."*
*We were a family of four girls and were all
trained in piano. A busy household with a
schedule of who could practice when with five of
us playing. Years later found myself and my*

---

[20] "A 'Healing' Return to the Home of Songwriter Ruth Lowe," Dave LeBlanc,
The Globe and Mail, June 2018, see https://www.theglobeandmail.com/real-
estate/toronto/article-a-healing-return-to-the-home-of-songwriter-ruth-lowe/.

husband transferred to Winnipeg. I had time to fill and found myself in a music shop looking for music to—you guessed it—"I'll Never Smile Again"! It gave me such pleasure and changed my classical background to "Oldies but Goodies" and always with Dad in mind.

Years later my husband passed away (2016), and my pain was comforted in time at the piano playing "I'll Never Smile Again." It was not until today reading about you and Ruth Lowe, that I came to know the story behind the music. It just resonated in so many ways—so poignant—just as the music. So, thank you for sharing your wonderful legacy.

Sincerely,
Jane Lindsay[21]

And here's yet another story to do with an amazing song. It's a sense of *déjà vu*. Let's let Canadian Jewish News writer Cynthia Gasner tell the tale from her 2012 column:[22]

Many Canadians do not know that one of the world's greatest pop songs of all time, "I'll Never Smile Again," was written by a Canadian, Ruth Lowe, more than 60 years ago. Although the song has been recorded by famous orchestras and well-known vocalists, it was not until recently (2004) that attention was once again focused on the composer. The original, four-page, hand-written manuscript turned up in Winnipeg and was returned to Lowe's son, Toronto photographer, Tom Sandler.

---

[21] Reprinted with permission from Jane Lindsay.
[22] Reprinted with permission from Cynthia Gasner.

"Although she won a Grammy Award and her music was No. 1 for months, and is still heard regularly, I think she has never been recognized properly in her own country," says Sandler. "She was a pioneer in the music industry, worked with many of the greats and has produced something that lives on."

Lowe wrote "I'll Never Smile Again" in 1939, to express her grief after the death of her first husband, music publicist, Harold Cohen, at the age of 29. She had given the original manuscript to her friend Vida Guthrie, who was the musical arranger for orchestra leader Percy Faith.

Guthrie died in 1990, and the music sheets went to her daughter, Jane Morton, who lives in Winnipeg. Morton did not know what to do with the manuscript (for many years, keeping it in her piano bench where it almost met an untimely end due to a flood: fortunately, she rescued it in time).

This summer, Morton received a call from a friend who told her that the History Channel was going to show a documentary biography on Lowe, who died in 1981 at 66. After she saw Lowe's son, Tom, on the program, she got his e-mail address and sent him a note telling him that she had his mother's original manuscript.

OK, Tom Sandler takes over the story from here...

"There have been many magical and wonderful moments in my life, and this was one of them. When Jane Morton contacted me, what she said stopped me in my tracks: 'Your mom, Ruth, gave my mom, Vida, a copy of the handwritten 'I'll Never Smile Again' manuscript as a gift. For all these years, it's been in the piano bench in our home in Winnipeg. I've been waiting all this time to return it to your family but didn't know where or how to do that.'"

Figure 47: I'll Never Smile Again original manuscript

"I was deeply moved to hear this. Jane told me about the flood in the basement where the piano was: the water rose to just under the piano bench and no further, so all the music was safe. Jane also said she almost got in touch with the Sinatra family, thinking perhaps they should have it, but something told her to hang on to it. I was overwhelmed and booked a flight the next day to Winnipeg. Jane was waiting for me at the airport, as well as a CBC cameraman and reporter. She handed me the envelope, I opened it, and pulled out the score. The first thing I recognized was my mom's crazy handwriting, I knew it was the real thing, no question! The reporter asked me how I felt, and I remember replying, 'I think I'll Smile Again.'"

We went back to the Morton's home where they were so gracious and kind. I stayed for the day and caught the late flight back to Toronto with this priceless manuscript in hand. You know, I felt so close to my mom as I held it. It was part of her heart that now had come home to rest. Thank you so much, Jane, for what you did and for the gift you gave us."

Now, if you haven't been to Toronto's famed Casa Loma, you owe it to yourself to correct that. Spanish for "Hill House," we're talking a Gothic Revival-style mansion that was constructed in the early years of the 20th century as a residence for financier Sir Henry Pellatt.

It's here that singer-songwriter Sean Jones brings his "Soul in the City" gig, playing outside in the glass pavilion found amongst the beautiful gardens of Casa Loma. Each evening's a sell-out with up to 2,000 people attending.

"I decided to write some retro soul music and not worry about making it more modern to try to please a younger audience," he says. "I have a new sense of confidence that is helping me to feel secure in the decisions that I'm making artistically."

And believe it or not, that confidence has taken him to the music of Ruth Lowe.

Figure 48: Sean Jones

"I'd never heard the song," Sean says. "I'd never heard of Ruth Lowe. But then I met Tom and he told me about it, and so I started listening to different versions. It was Billie Holiday's interpretation that really struck me. And I remember saying, 'Oh wow! This is something. This is a beautiful song.' And I started trying to sing it. It wasn't until I actually started to sing it that I said, 'Man, this is a *gorgeous* song!' So, then I brought it to the band, and they played it so beautifully and we did it for the first time here, at 'Soul in the City'."

"Christian did a gorgeous big band arrangement of it," says Miles Raine, saxophonist in Sean's group, referring to the trombone player who scores many of their sets. "I'd actually heard the song before, but I never connected how important it was. The whole story of the song was important. I mean, a Jewish woman, in 1939, and the world's going to hell in a hand basket, and she turns around and writes a song dealing with her grief. I just can't get enough of that story."

"Then, we arrive at tonight," says Sean, "where we've got a 26-piece orchestra with strings and flutes and everything. And I just knew we needed to do 'I'll Never Smile Again' with this amazing band."

Indeed, it was stunning.

Before Sean sang the tune, Tom Sandler got up in front of the crowd and briefly explained the significance of the song without mentioning Ruth. When he came to the end of his dissertation, finally stating it had been written by his mother, there was an audible gasp in the crowd.

"I had tears in my eyes with you talking about this," Sean tells Tom after the show. "The way you told the story was perrrrrfect!! I mean, everybody was just like...oh man...a collective gasp out of the audience! It's this honest, sincere passion you have for this story. That's what got me to listen to the actual song. And, you know, it's simple, this song. What it's saying. Simple words and beautiful music. That's what makes it. It hits you. It's honest. And that's the mark of a great song. I'm in love with that song, man. It's such a great tune: it's all there!"

Chapter Seventeen

CODA: A Canadian Musical Heroine

*Coda: an expanded cadence that brings a
piece of music to an end.*

But some things never end.

Frank Sinatra—the star whose career exploded overnight with Ruth's song—knew the value of a winner. He re-recorded "I'll Never Smile Again" with the Gordon Jenkins orchestra in the 1950s, and again in the 1960s, and again in the 1970s. In fact, he sang the song up to the end of his performing life.

"I'll Never Smile Again"—and Ruth's life—endured also with the stage show "Ruthie," employing several of her songs and staged by Tom Kneebone and Dinah Christie. Produced by the Smile Theatre Company of Toronto, the production serves to bring luminescence to Ruth Lowe's incredible accomplishments.

The resplendent Dinah Christie, brilliant and dazzling as always, is welcoming at her 100-acre spread in Grey County, Ontario. "I bought it in 1971 for $16,000. That was a lot of money back then." The scenery getting here has been stunning, complete with sprawling fields of luminous rapeseed and Mennonite horse drawn buggies making their way amidst the common people steering their motorized vehicles in and around Holstein, "the little village with a huge heart." This community is home to some of the county's most popular events: Holstein Maplefest, Holstein Rodeo Expo, and, of course, who could forget the famous Holstein Non-Motorized Santa Claus Parade!

While the surrounding region is known for being leisurely, Dinah has no intention of slowing down. She is actively working with a Vancouver producer to mount a staged production revolving around the songs of Dame Vera Lynn who is still held in great affection by veterans of the Second World War for the songs that has her cited "the Briton who best exemplified the spirit of the 20th century." Ms. Lynn is also notable for being the only artist to have a span on the British single and album charts reaching from their inception to the 21st century. It's impossible to write about her without hearing "We'll Meet Again" and "The White Cliffs of Dover" echoing in your mind, so engrained is her fame worldwide.

But, much as Dinah Christie's resilience is clearly a force to be reckoned with as she readies herself to fly to Vancouver for meetings, today's journey has a more immediate purpose: to harken back to 1990 when *Ruthie* was staged by the Smile Theatre, the performing entity established in 1972 to enrich the lives of seniors by presenting meaningful, well-crafted, professional performances created just for them. As the Smile team is proud to say, "We do our work each year with diligence—consistently, expertly, often unnoticed by the mainstream, and with passion. Our biggest accomplishment? Our commitment to the highest quality performances, no matter how small the space we perform in, or whatever the circumstances."

"It was TK's baby, of course," Dinah exclaims. "And I was along to help out with the production wherever I could."

TK—or "Teeks," as she lovingly refers to the late Tom Kneebone—is best remembered as one of Canada's favourite cabaret performers and actors. Born in Auckland, New Zealand, Tom studied at the Bristol Old Vic Theatre School in England, eventually moving to Canada in 1963 and performing in various Canadian revues, often with Dinah as his onstage partner and offstage associate producer. Kneebone's Order of Canada honour is in recognition of being a "multi-talented performer who has had a long and eclectic career," while his Order of Ontario reflects having "brought joy to the lives of thousands of seniors confined to nursing homes and long-term care facilities through live theatre." It's clear Dinah misses their close association.

Figure 49: Ruthie program cover

"I think it was 1987 when Teeks became Artistic Director of the Smile Theatre," she says. "I so wish he were here to tell you about *Ruthie*. We had a wonderful actress in the lead role, and she did such a lovely job, talking directly to the audience, and carrying on about this and that. You know, we staged *Ruthie* to appreciative audiences for a solid month."

Dinah can't recall the name of that actress from almost 30 years ago. But a few days later, she has a *déjà vu* moment and calls: "It was Barbara Fulton! That's who the actress was who played Ruth. She was amazing!"

"I didn't even audition," Barbara explains from her home in Stratford, Ontario, reaching back to the time she played Ruth Lowe on the stage. "Dinah and Tom had seen me perform on stage in *Cats* and so they accepted I could sing and act, and they just 'knew' I could play Ruth. They simply offered me the role without an audition."

"Ruthie" would hit the stage as a one-woman show, Barbara playing Ruth Lowe and talking directly to the audience about her life and times, telling a story about her musical history, including reflecting on the death of her first husband and how that became the inspiration for "I'll Never Smile Again."

"Everyone was experiencing grief about the outset of war overseas," Barbara says, "and they tried to shut down such unhappiness. But it was that wonderful song that Ruth wrote that gave them permission for the emotion to come out and be expressed.

"There were sad parts to the show, obviously," says Barbara, "but the actor's job is not to cry but create an opportunity for the audience to have tears if they wish. And the audiences knew all of her music. Of course, we included other music of the times, so we'd play things that Ina Ray Hutton had done, that kind of thing. Our goal was that Ruth would be the conduit to enliven the people in the audience who we knew would remember the music of the times. That was the focus: Ruth in the 1940s, but not her later life. Of course, we mentioned how 'I'll Never Smile Again' put Sinatra on the map.

"We had a little tiny prop piano on casters that I pretended to play," Barbara continues, "and I was able to wheel it around the stage to different spots to make it more interesting as I told my stories. So, I was basically a storyteller, with Ruth's music and other tunes of the '40s holding it together. For sure, it was a nostalgic trip down memory lane for the people I was playing to. And it was such an honour to have the role of Ruth Lowe: a Canadian legend."

Barbara knew a bit about Ruth because of being in Charlottetown, PEI in the early 1980s, doing a show produced by

Alan Lund called *Singin' and Dancin' Tonight*. It featured Canadian music and included "I'll Never Smile Again." Because the performers were Canadian and the show featured the music of Canadian composers, each singer did their own research to find out some background on the songs they sang. "So, I did learn something about Ruth Lowe," Barbara says, "and because of that, she wasn't a brand-new person to me when I started doing *Ruthie*. I knew how incredible she was."

Still, Barbara didn't have any footage of Ruth speaking or doing things, so she would have to delve into the actors' trunk to invent what she thought Ruth would have talked like, based on who she was and what her mannerisms were.

"I tried to honour her story and tell it authentically," Barbara says. "And I think we achieved that. We got rave reviews from all the audiences we played to, that's for sure. The audience reaction: that's what made it all worthwhile. They knew all the songs, but they'd literally come up and sit down beside me or dance, so it became an interactive show sometimes. It was amazing. I loved it: it was so cool.

"And you know what: it stayed with me for a long time after we were done," recalls Barbara. "What had happened to Ruth and the great celebration and celebrity that visited her...you don't just shake that off when you're done acting. She was incredible, an amazing lady. But it seems so little is known about her: why is she not celebrated more in Canada? I mean, there's a Grammy with her name on it from the U.S. but not a Juno here. That's crazy. It would be such a shame that this incredibly talented lady might be forgotten in her own country."

Not to worry that the famed songwriter's story has not been totally overlooked. Ruth's life was chronicled in the video documentary *I'll Never Smile Again: The Ruth Lowe Story*, produced by Great North Productions. It was broadcast on CBC as part of the television series *The Canadians*.[23]

---

[23] https://www.youtube.com/watch?v=B_CjpVbRZYc.

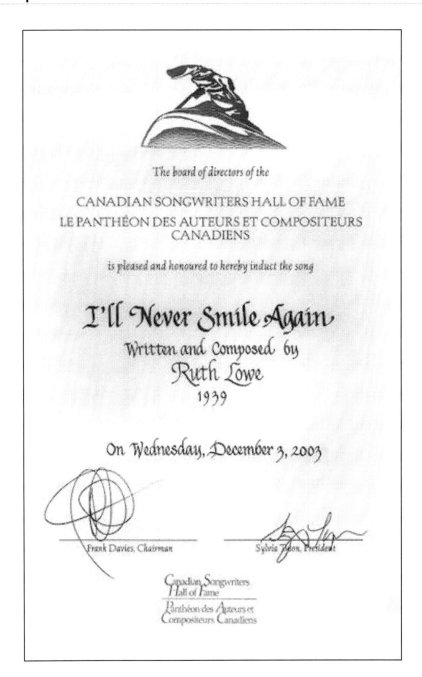

Figure 50: Canadian Songwriters Hall of Fame

41 Valleybrook Drive
Toronto ON Canada M3B 2S6
T 416.442.3816 F 416.442.3831
www.cshf.ca

Wednesday, February 18, 2015

E-mail: tsandler1@ca.inter.net

Mr. Tom Sandler
119 Wembley Rd
Toronto, Ontario M6C-2G5

Dear Tom:

Canadian Songwriters Hall of Fame 2015 Song Induction – *Put Your Dreams Away (For Another Day)*

I am pleased to inform you that the song, *Put Your Dreams Away (For Another Day)*, co-written by your late musical mother, Ruth Lowe, has been selected for induction into the Canadian Songwriters Hall of Fame (CSHF). This classic song demonstrates excellence in the art of songwriting and has made an outstanding contribution to Canadian music.

In honour of your mother's achievement, a page on our website (www.cshf.ca) will be dedicated to *Put Your Dreams Away (For Another Day)*, including a bio and popular audio recording of the song, photos, and lyrics. We would be delighted if you would contribute to this song page by providing photographs, personal insights, additional information about the story of the song, etc. As well, you will receive a CSHF Song Induction Certificate which will be couriered to you in due course. Please note that applicable parties for co-writers Paul Mann and Stephan Weiss have also been notified of the song's induction into the Hall of Fame.

Put Your Dreams Away (For Another Day) will be publically celebrated via "Covered Classics", a new element in the CSHF's song induction program. A collaboration between the CSHF and CBC/Radio-Canada, this series involves having newly inducted songs covered by Canadian musical talent. A beautiful acoustic rendition, performed by Alejandra Ribera, will be featured on CBC/Radio Canada and CSHF platforms. We hope that this cover will introduce your mother's classic song to an entirely new generation of music lovers. Content is scheduled to be released on cshf.ca, CBCMusic.ca and ICIMusique.ca on March 2, 2015.

Should you be interested in contributing to the song page, wish to be notified of related broadcasts and media coverage, or have any further questions, please contact Lisa Gaglia, Manager, CSHF (Phone: 416-442-3816 / E-mail: gaglia@cshf.ca). Lisa may also be in touch with you if the opportunity for a related media interview arises.

Congratulations once again on your mother's incredible achievement. We are proud to have *Put Your Dreams Away (For Another Day)* inducted into the Canadian Songwriters Hall of Fame.

Sincerely,

Stan Meissner
Chair, Board of Directors

*Figure 51: Canadian Songwriters Induction Letter for
Put Your Dreams Away*

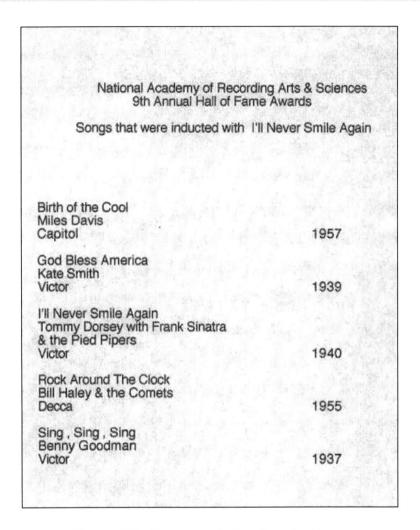

National Academy of Recording Arts & Sciences
9th Annual Hall of Fame Awards

Songs that were inducted with I'll Never Smile Again

Birth of the Cool
Miles Davis
Capitol   1957

God Bless America
Kate Smith
Victor   1939

I'll Never Smile Again
Tommy Dorsey with Frank Sinatra
& the Pied Pipers
Victor   1940

Rock Around The Clock
Bill Haley & the Comets
Decca   1955

Sing , Sing , Sing
Benny Goodman
Victor   1937

Figure 52: Grammy Induction Letter

Meanwhile, Tom Sandler has not given up on a desire to see his mother's reputation immortalized. "I'll Never Smile Again" was inducted into the Canadian Songwriters Hall of Fame in 2003, with "Put Your Dreams Away" following in 2015. Indeed, Ruth Lowe was the inspiration behind Frank Davies, the organization's Chair, creating the CSHF in the first place. Tom's also been working with the Juno Awards that honour Canadian music achievement to have her commemorated. "Whether it's a special achievement award named after her," he says, "or another form of recognition, it needs to happen. I mean, how come the Grammys have recognized her but we haven't even done that in her own country? It's not right. So many great Canadians who deserve to be inducted and recognized but who have not been yet, Mom being one of them."

By the way, it should be noted that Ruth shared stellar company the night her work was posthumously recognized by the Grammys. Frank Sinatra led the nomination for his old friend. Joining "I'll Never Smile Again" was Benny Goodman's immortal jazz ground breaker "Sing, Sing, Sing," the early rock 'n roll single "Rock around The Clock" by Bill Haley and the Comets, Kate Smith's anthemic "God Bless America," and Miles Davis' influential "Birth of the Cool." Not bad company to keep!

"Our family didn't get any advance notice of the induction," says Tom. "My dad and brother were both out of town and we were stuck in Toronto. Funnily enough, though, we all watched the Grammys that night from various locations, and we all saw it. Another great honour for my mom and our family."

Today, Ruth Lowe *is* remembered. Her renown as a musical giant of the 20th century is firm.

Her greatest tragedy in life won her a triumphant career and the respect and adoration of thousands of people worldwide.

To Tommy Sandler goes this concluding dispatch:

"My mom's life was one of contrasts: deep sorrow and great celebrations. She loved to live, she loved having parties, helping charities, giving gifts, planting trees, playing her piano most of all. She loved her family and friends. She was a kind, giving person. There isn't one individual I've ever met who wasn't crazy about her, everyone from the greatest songwriters and performers in music history, to the shopkeepers on Eglinton Avenue in Toronto where we grew up. She had a quality and charm about her, she'd make you feel good when she was around. She always brought the sun. In fact, she used to tease me as a kid: if I was unhappy and sulking on a cloudy day, she'd say, 'Tommy, know what? If you smile, the sun will shine.' And, sure enough, I'd smile, and, sure enough, the sun would come out."

"She had magic about her, the magic that only love and belief can bring, magic of the heart. She wasn't afraid to share it and to celebrate the joy of life. Her music was her secret language, the bridge between her pain and loneliness. It connected her with the world, it lifted her up, and healed her wounds. Her music, so powerful, it could mend a broken heart. In fact, it was once said, 'I'll Never Smile Again' is on the same level of music as 'How Can You Heal a Broken Heart' by the Bee Gees.' Now, that's so true. And it does put things in perspective."

Figure 53: Tommy, Ruth, Nat, Stephen 1963

"I want the world to know what Mom left as a legacy. Frankly, the great gift she gave to me was life-changing: turning me on to the joy of music, the joy of being creative. And the happiness and the freedom and the hope that gave me and gives me to this day. It was a big, very powerful package...amazing. It hit me like a tidal wave. She knew she could communicate with me on a very deep level and a very broad experiential level. I'm not sure my dad was fulfilling that dimension but when she discovered I was, well, there was this communications thing between us that became very serious, very powerful. And she needed to pass that on. And I am so fortunate to have been there to receive it."

"I think her music made a lot of people feel really good. I do a presentation about her in different places, and people tell me that they met each other through that song, they fell in love to that song and to that music, and they're still in love and they're still married. Even younger people, sitting there, listening and holding hands. That's what it's really all about. It's about a certain kind of intimacy and love and companionship and the human experience and the beating of the heart and expressing it and being alive and just feeling complete."

"Her music always lifted me up higher. She always was able to take me, no matter if I was down or just concerned about things, she could just sit down at the piano and it would just take over everything. It would take you to another place, to a better place, where there was hope, and there was something to believe in. What a great legacy she has left."

"It's the heart and the soul of this whole book."

And if that bespeaks the brilliance of Ruth Lowe's life—a young lady who had prematurely concluded she would never smile again—so be it.

RESOURCES

You may be interested to know more about Ruth Lowe. There is lots available to scan on Google, along with watching the documentary "I'll Never Smile Again: The Ruth Lowe Story" produced by Great North Productions.[24]

And here's a great treasure trove for you. Go to www.untilismileatyou.com/ and click on "Treasures." There you will find a vast array of scans and audio files that showcase the amazing life of Ruth Lowe. We're talking telegrams from noted celebrities, copies of Ruth's original song sheets, record labels... it's all there and we invite you to partake. Use the password "Ruth" if called to do so.

[24] https://www.bing.com/videos/search?q=the+canadians+youtube+ruth+lowe &&view=detail&mid=395E0A2926D073B8B660395E0A2926D073B8B660 &&FORM=VRDGAR.

ACKNOWLEDGEMENTS

Thank you to the many, many supporters of this project who have aided us in seeking details about Ruth Lowe's life. Thanks also for spurring us on when the walls threatened to hold us back. Some facts seemed lost to history, but through patient investigation and great assistance, we were able to re-build old files.

Castle Carrington's star Editor, Margot Wilson, performed a wonderful, and speedy, editing job and I can't thank you enough. You make this book look superb, Margot.

Work on this project could not have been completed without the good friends and Beta Test Readers who gave of their time to help determine if we had a worthwhile book on our hands. Fortunately, their responses were keen for "Until I Smile At You." Thanks to each of you, especially for catching those typos!

And also, to the many people interviewed for this book: thank *you* so much. Your stories—and your preparedness to share them—make this a resourceful and inspirational treasure.

I had a wonderful time talking with author James Kaplan on March 7th, 2016. His biographies, *Sinatra: The Voice* and *Sinatra: The Chairman* are treasure troves of information, published by Anchor (part of the Knopf Doubleday Publishing Group). James and I talked at length about Sinatra, Dorsey, and, of course, the mastery of Ruth Lowe. Thanks, James, for allowing me to reproduce parts of our discussion and quote from your books in order to broaden the story.

My thanks also to Mark Steyn for his appraisal of the Dorsey/Sinatra recording covered in "I'll Never Smile Again" featured online and in his book, *A Song For The Season* published by Stockade Books.

The late Peter Levinson revealed facts about Tommy Dorsey in his book *Tommy Dorsey: Livin' In A Great Big Way* and I thank his publisher, Da Capo Press, part of the Hachette Publishing Group, for their permission to cite passages.

Dave LeBlanc is a talented journalist working for the *Globe and Mail* newspaper. Thanks, Dave, for allowing us to reproduce part of the wonderful column you wrote, "A 'Healing' Return to the Home of Songwriter Ruth Lowe."

Thanks also to Cynthia Gasner for permitting us to reproduce part of her column from the *Canadian Jewish News*.

And to Amanda Erlinger, Nancy Sinatra's daughter: thank you so much, Amanda, for helping us secure that wonderful photo of your mom and grandfather that we used in the Foreword.

Cheers,
Peter Jennings

ABOUT THE AUTHORS

Peter Jennings
Photo credit, Rosie Leeson

Peter Jennings is a well-known author having written several books, including:

Shark Assault: An Amazing Story of Survival (with Nicole Moore)
www.sharkassault.com
Riveting and inspirational… a compelling real life story about the magnificent power of optimism.
Lloyd Robertson, longest serving news anchor in television history

Being Happy Matters

www.beinghappymatters.life

Peter, I think it's brilliant that you're writing this book because people are so down, and they do need to think about happiness.

Allan Fotheringham, author, columnist, humourist

Pushing The Boundaries: How To Get More Out of Life

www.pushingtheboundaries.life

"Pushing the Boundaries" should be on everyone's "must read" list for this year. It's an inspired and inspiring work. Peter Jennings is a master at attracting diverse, unique interviewees and "Pushing the Boundaries" is no exception. It will renew your faith in humanity.

Cindy Watson, author of *Out of Darkness: The Jeff Healey Story*

Behind The Seams

www.marilynbrooks.com

I lapped up Marilyn's engaging memoirs, written with great charm and candor. Her colorful stories are rife with drama and daring and serve as a sweet style ticket back to a time of innocence and idealism.

Jeanne Beker, television personality, fashion editor, columnist, and author

For Want Of 40 Pounds
www.forwantof40pounds.com

Bert Mann's descriptions of appalling deprivations and impersonal brutality of the Nazi invasion and his epic escape at the age of 14 to walk 700 miles and then stow away to reach England... is nothing short of a miracle.
Dianne Lang, author of *Saving Mandela's Children*

He is currently researching/writing several more. You can learn more at www.peterjennings.me.

Tom Sandler

Photo credit, Aline Sandler

Tom Sandler is a well-known photographer in Toronto who regularly photographs international people of prominence. Having worked on the International Duke of Edinburgh Awards, hosted by Prince Philip, he has moved on to photograph other royals such as Prince Edward and his wife Sophie, including taking the shot they used for their Christmas card.

Tom has captured the images of many members of Toronto's social set as well as international celebrities and politicians like Nelson Mandela, Margaret Thatcher, and the Rolling Stones.

You can see Tom's photo gallery at
https://tomsandler.photoshelter.com/gallery-list.

Manufactured by Amazon.ca
Bolton, ON